the SEWING BIBLE
SLIPCOVERS

SERIES EDITOR **WENDY GARDINER**

the SEWING BIBLE
SLIPCOVERS

SERIES EDITOR **WENDY GARDINER**

D&C
David and Charles

A DAVID & CHARLES BOOK
Copyright © David & Charles Limited 2010

David & Charles is an F+W Media Inc. company
4700 East Galbraith Road
Cincinnati, OH 45236

First published in the UK in 2010

Text copyright © Wendy Gardiner 2010
Photography, designs and artwork © David & Charles 2010

ISBN-13: 978-0-7153-3042-5 paperback
ISBN-10: 0-7153-3042-X paperback

Printed in China by RR Donnelley
for David & Charles
Brunel House   Newton Abbot   Devon

Acquisitions Editor: Jennifer Fox-Proverbs
Editor: Bethany Dymond
Assistant Editor: Kate Nicholson
Project Editor: Karen Hemingway
Design Manager: Sarah Clark
Creative Manager: Prudence Rogers
Production Controller: Beverley Richardson
Photographer: Simon Whitmore

www.davidandcharles.co.uk

David & Charles publish high quality books on a wide range of subjects.
For more great book ideas visit:
www.rubooks.co.uk

CONTENTS

INTRODUCTION   6

BASIC EQUIPMENT AND MATERIALS   8
BASIC TECHNIQUES   14
FABRIC   24

TRIMMING SLIPCOVERS   30

glitzy cushion cover   34

MAKING BUTTONS, TIES AND STRAP FASTENINGS   38

kitsch kitchen chair cushion   42

EMBELLISHING WITH APPLIQUÉ   46

designer director's chair   52

SEWING CURVED SEAMS AND ADDING BINDINGS   58

delicious dining style   62

MAKING RUFFLES AND TUCKS   68

seriously stylish seating   72

MAKING AND INSERTING PIPING   76

box clever bench seating   80

INSERTING ZIPPERS   84

soft and squishy beanbag   88

DECORATIVE STITCHING AND SURFACE EMBELLISHMENT   92

handsome headboard   96

MAKING PLEATS   102

beautiful tailored bedspread   106

SEWING SPECIAL SEAMS   112

designer laundry basket liner   116

WORKING WITH PATTERNED FABRIC   120

contemporary classic chair cover   124

MAKING SLIP-ON CHAIR COVERS   128

fabulous fitted chair cover   134

GLOSSARY   138
TEMPLATES   142
FABRIC SUPPLIERS AND CONTRIBUTORS   143
ABOUT THE AUTHOR   143
INDEX   144

Introduction

WELCOME TO SEWING BIBLE, SLIPCOVERS — YOU'VE TAKEN THE FIRST STEP TO HAVING FUN WITH FURNISHINGS! ADDING OR REPLACING SLIPCOVERS IS AN EXCELLENT WAY TO UPDATE YOUR DÉCOR AND, OF COURSE, IT CAN BE VERY COST EFFECTIVE TOO. IT'S ALSO A GREAT WAY TO BE CREATIVE AND ADVENTUROUS WITH YOUR HOME STYLING AS EACH ROOM CAN BE FURNISHED TO SUIT YOUR PERSONALITY AND INDIVIDUAL PREFERENCES.

THIS BOOK INCLUDES ALL THE BASIC INFORMATION REQUIRED TO GET STARTED, FIRST EXPLAINING THE EQUIPMENT YOU NEED AND PROBABLY HAVE ALREADY, AND HOW TO CHOOSE FABRICS, AS WELL AS HOW TO MASTER THE BASIC TECHNIQUES. YOU WILL SEE THAT THE PROJECTS GET SLIGHTLY MORE COMPLEX THROUGH THE BOOK, SO IF YOU ARE AN ABSOLUTE BEGINNER, START WITH THE SIMPLE CUSHIONS, DIRECTOR'S CHAIR AND TABLECLOTH. EACH PROJECT IS PRECEDED BY A SECTION EXPLAINING NEW TECHNIQUES THAT WILL NOT ONLY HELP WITH THE PROJECT, BUT ALSO INCREASE YOUR REPERTOIRE FOR FUTURE MAKES. ALL THE WAY THROUGH THE BOOK, YOU WILL FIND EXPERT TIPS AND SEWING SENSE SUGGESTIONS THAT MAKE IT EASIER TO COMPLETE THE PROJECTS AND CREATE A UNIQUE STYLE FOR YOUR OWN HOME.

THE PROJECTS ALL INCLUDE A MATERIALS LIST
AS WELL AS ILLUSTRATED STEP-BY-STEP
INSTRUCTIONS, SO WHETHER YOU ARE A NOVICE
SEWER OR KEEN SEAMSTER, SEWING BIBLE,
SLIPCOVERS HAS SOMETHING FOR YOU!

ENJOY, AND CREATE HOME FURNISHINGS THAT
ARE JUST SO YOU!

BASIC EQUIPMENT AND MATERIALS

TO MAKE SLIPCOVERS SUCCESSFULLY,
ALL YOU NEED ARE A FEW ITEMS OF
BASIC EQUIPMENT, WHICH YOU WILL
PROBABLY ALREADY HAVE IN YOUR
SEWING KIT. ARMED WITH THESE,
YOU WILL BE READY TO TACKLE A
WIDE RANGE OF PROJECTS WITH
COMPLETE CONFIDENCE.

MAKE SURE YOU KEEP YOUR
EQUIPMENT IN THE BEST
CONDITION SO THAT YOU CAN
PRODUCE REALLY PROFESSIONAL
RESULTS. ALWAYS INVEST IN THE
BEST QUALITY YOU CAN AFFORD
AND, IF YOU ARE TEMPTED, THERE
ARE VARIOUS ADDITIONAL TOOLS
AVAILABLE THAT WILL SAVE YOU
TIME AND EFFORT.

BASIC SEWING KIT

This kit is recommended for making
all your slipcovers, including the
projects in this book. You will find
more detail on which types to choose
on the following pages.
- ✓ Sewing machine and needles
- ✓ Shears and scissors
- ✓ Long, glass-headed pins
- ✓ Marking tool
- ✓ General-purpose thread
- ✓ Tape measure, metre (yard) stick,
set square

SEWING MACHINE

Although you can, of course, sew by hand, it is far quicker
to make slipcovers with a sewing machine. A basic
machine with straight and zigzag stitch is all that is needed,
but one that can drop the feed dogs is a good idea if you
want to try free motion stitching (see pp. 94–95).

Make sure your machine is in good working order and that
you have a good understanding of how it works, using the
manufacturer's manual for guidance. You will need various
feet and a selection of needles to use with your machine.

 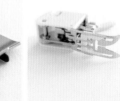

ZIPPER FOOT   BLIND HEM FOOT   WALKING FOOT

SEWING MACHINE FEET

The **general purpose** or **straight stitch foot** is the basic foot that comes with the machine and is suitable for all general purposes such as sewing seams.

A **zipper foot** is useful for piping as well as for inserting zippers. It usually has a thinner centre with grooves either side so that you can stitch close to the zipper teeth or piping cord.

A **walking foot** will help feed the top and bottom fabrics evenly as you sew. This is particularly useful for pattern matching and when sewing thick plush fabrics such as fleece or velvet.

A **blind hem foot** often has a thin metal strip extending below the foot, which is used to butt against the folded hem. The blind hemstitch, found on most modern sewing machines, will stitch straight stitch within the hem allowance and a regularly spaced but occasional zigzag stitch into the main fabric, thus securing the hem in place. All that is visible from the right side of the fabric is a very tiny ladder stitch.

A **pin tuck foot** has grooves on the underside and is used in conjunction with a twin needle to stitch uniform pin tucks quickly. The number of grooves determines how many pin tucks you can stitch closely together in parallel lines at the same time. The fabric slots into the centre groove under the twin needles, which simultaneously stitch parallel rows of stitching on each side of the tuck.

A BASIC SEWING MACHINE WITH STRAIGHT AND ZIGZAG STITCH IS ALL YOU REALLY NEED TO SEW SLIPCOVERS SUCCESSFULLY.

A **cording foot** also has a groove underneath through which cord is fed as you stitch over it. This helps to keep the cord in the correct position as you zigzag stitch from side to side.

You may also find other specialist presser feet helpful. For example, a darning foot is useful for free-motion stitching (see pp. 94–95) and an invisible zipper foot makes the job of inserting zippers invisibly very easy (see pp. 86–87).

MACHINE NEEDLES

When sewing most soft furnishing fabrics, choose a robust needle: sizes 12–14 (80–90 European) for medium-weight fabrics and sizes 16–18 (100–110) for heavyweight fabrics. For very heavy fabrics, use a size 20 (120) needle. For lightweight voiles, a size 9–11 (60–75) is suitable.

Remember to change the needle with every new project. A blunt needle can cause skipped stitches, broken thread and even holes or snags in the fabric. Always have a supply of spare needles to hand so that you can replace broken needles quickly.

EXPERT TIP

IF A SEAM PUCKERS, THE NEEDLE MAY BE TOO BIG, SO TRY A SMALLER ONE. IF THE NEEDLE OR THREAD BREAKS, THE NEEDLE MAY BE TOO SMALL, SO TRY A BIGGER ONE.

PIN TUCK FEET

CORDING FOOT

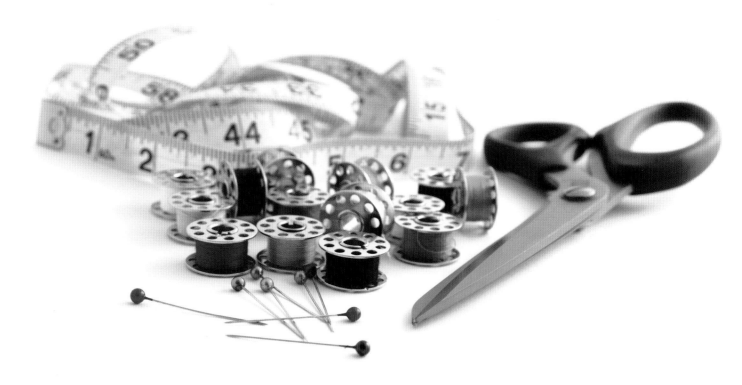

SHARP, GOOD QUALITY DRESSMAKING SHEARS AND LONG PINS ARE ESSENTIALS ITEMS OF KIT.

SCISSORS

Dressmaking shears

You can recognise shears by the moulded handles, the larger hole for your fingers and a smaller one for your thumb. They are available for right- and left-handed use, with the moulded handles appropriately shaped. Make sure your shears are good quality with long straight blades so you can cut smoothly. Keep the blades sharp and never use them for anything other than cutting fabric.

Some dressmaking shears have very fine serrated edges along the cutting blades, which help to grip the fabric as it is cut. Others have soft-touch handles that are slightly spongy and useful if you are cutting large quantities at a time because they are gentler on the hand. Spring-loaded scissors, with handles one on top of the other, are also available. They spring open between cuts, making them easier to use if your hands suffer from arthritis.

Dressmaking scissors

A pair of dressmaking scissors is handy for clipping into seam allowances, cutting threads and also cutting smaller curves and notches.

Seam rippers

Also known as quick-unpicks, these often come with sewing machines. They have a hooked blade with a pointed end, which is slipped under stitches and pushed through to cut the thread. They are also very handy for cutting open buttonholes. Take care to use a seam ripper in a controlled manner and ensure that you are not cutting anything you did not anticipate.

Rotary cutters

A rotary cutter has a circular blade attached to a handle. It must be used on a self-healing cutting mat, and a long cutting ruler is also useful. Cutters can simply be rolled along a cutting line to cut through fabric and are ideal for large projects with straight edges. Some cutters have blades that can be safely retracted when not in use or alternative blades with different cutting effects such as fluted edges. Remember that the sharp cutter is a potential hazard and store it safely.

Pinking shears

These have serrated edges and make a zigzag cut edge, which helps to prevent the fabric fraying. They can be used to neatened edges of lightweight cottons and poly/cotton fabrics quickly and easily. They are also useful for cutting interfacing.

PINS

Long glass-headed or flower-headed pins are ideal for making soft furnishings. Place them at right angles to the seam so they can be removed easily as you sew. Replace blunt pins regularly to avoid them snagging fabric. Remember that should they come into contact with heat, from an iron for example, any plastic heads on pins will melt. You could also use quilting safety pins for pinning layers of fabric together.

SEWING SENSE
When cutting out delicate fabrics that might be marked by pins, use fabric weights (or even clean tin cans) instead of pins to stop the fabric shifting.

THREADS

Use a good quality general-purpose polyester-covered cotton thread for most projects. Of course, you can opt to use silk threads on delicate silk fabrics and pure cotton thread with cotton or linen fabric. Choose a thread colour that matches the fabric. If you can't find an exact match, it is better to go slightly darker with the thread. For patterned fabric, match the background or most prominent colour.

MEASURING TOOLS

A good quality **tape measure** is essential. One that shows metric and imperial measurements on the same side is ideal. Easier for long lengths, a straight **metre (yard) stick** can be used to measure and mark curtain lengths quickly.

An accurate large **set square**, such as a carpenters' square, is ideal for giving you a perfect right angle. The two rulers or outer edges will help you ensure that fabric is straight both vertically (lengthwise) and horizontally (crosswise).

A **French curve** is a curved measuring tool, which is very useful for marking out and drawing curves. They are either a length of bendy plastic or a flat, hard plastic shape with different curved areas and markings.

MARKING TOOLS

A selection of marking tools is useful. They all have different advantages, so choose the type to suit your project and a colour to show up on your fabric.

Chalk markers are convenient to use because chalk is easily removed once it has served its purpose. They are available in different forms. A **chalk wheel** deposits a very fine line of loose chalk as you run the wheel along the line to be marked. Different colours of loose chalk are available in pre-packed containers. **Chalk pencils** usually come in packs of two colours, white and pink or blue, to use on light or dark fabric. Some are propelling pencils with tubes of different coloured chalk. A **chalk block**, contained in a plastic case, has a sharp edge so you can draw lines and make marks easily.

Marker pens come in a wide variety from permanent markers to water- or air-soluble pens. Vanishing or fade-away pens and pencils will fade after about 48 hours, so avoid using them if you plan to make a project over an extended period. Water-soluble pens are usually blue and the marks can be removed with a damp sponge or by washing. Do check how easily they are removed by checking on a scrap of fabric first.

PATTERN PAPER

Dressmaker's pattern paper comes in different weights and can be printed with ³⁄₈in (1cm) grid squares or with dots and crosses at 1in (2.5cm) intervals. The grid paper comes in packs and the dot and cross version is usually supplied on larger rolls. You could also make patterns on plain tracing paper, parcel paper or wallpaper lining.

SHEET MATERIALS

Occasionally you may wish to add interfacing, interlining or batting to a project to give it more body and greater strength. Use fusible web to bond two pieces of fabric together without stitching.

Pick an **interfacing** that suits the fabric being used. For instance, a medium-weight soft furnishing fabric will need a medium-weight interfacing. The idea is to add strength and stability without changing the handle of the fabric. There are sew-in and fusible varieties. **Sew-in interfacings** should be machine stitched to the wrong side of the fabric close to the edge all the way around.

Fusible interfacings are quick to use, but best avoided on fabrics with surface texture because you need to press well, which might flatten the surface of the fabric. Always press them to the wrong side of the fabric, lowering the iron onto the interfacing and pressing with a hot dry iron. Hold the iron in place for at least 10 seconds before lifting it off, moving to the next section and lowering it again. Do not glide the iron until the interfacing is securely in place. Once it is, allow the fabrics to cool before handling them again.

EXPERT TIP
CUT INTERFACING WITH PINKING SHEARS TO AVOID A PRONOUNCED HARD LINE.

Interlining is simply another layer of fabric, used to add bulk, weight and stability to the main fabric. It can be a lining fabric, cotton muslin or simply a toning lightweight cotton. Cut it to the same size as the main fabric and then sew them wrong sides together around the edges, ready to work with both layers as one.

Batting (wadding) is a soft spongy layer of material used to add bulk, particularly between layers of fabric to be quilted. Various thicknesses/weights of batting in polyester, cotton or silk are available and are generally bought by the yard (metre).

Fusible web is used to keep a hem in place without sewing. A double-sided version is also very useful for anchoring appliqué fabrics in place prior to stitching. Fuse the unprotected side of the web to the wrong side of the appliqué fabric. Then draw the design on the paper backing and cut out the fabric shape. Peel off the paper backing, position the appliqué on the main fabric and fuse it in place.

Fabric stabilizer is used to prevent the main fabric from puckering or distorting as it is stitched. There are a number of different types; the most common is a tear-away version, which is a good all-rounder. Place the stabilizer underneath the work and hoop it with the main fabric. Once stitched, tear the stabilizer away. Alternatives include soluble stabilizers, and iron-on and sticky stabilizers.

HANDY ACCESSORIES

A **point turner** looks like a short ruler, with one end angled to a point, which is used to push out corners fully. The measurements on the ruler also make this tool useful for accurately measuring and marking hems and side turnings.

A good quality steam **iron** is essential for any sewing project. When pressing, especially a delicate fabric or one with surface detail, always use a **pressing cloth** to protect the fabric. An ideal cloth is silk organza, which can withstand high temperatures and is transparent so you can see exactly what you are pressing.

EXPERT TIP
TO AVOID CRUSHING THE PILE ON A PLUSH FABRIC, USE A REMNANT OF THE SAME FABRIC AS A PRESSING CLOTH, PLACING THE TWO PILE TO PILE.

A **serger** is a very useful piece of equipment to own because it sews the seams, cuts off the seam allowance and overlocks the edges in one pass. Machines use from three to eight threads. However, a good pair of shears and the zigzag stitch on your sewing machine make sure that you achieve results that are just as serviceable.

BASIC TECHNIQUES

THERE ARE A FEW BASIC STITCHES AND SEWING TECHNIQUES THAT ARE HANDY TO KNOW BEFORE STARTING ON SOFT FURNISHINGS. THESE INCLUDE SOME GENERAL-PURPOSE HAND STITCHES, SIMPLE MACHINE STITCHING AND TECHNIQUES FOR SEAMING, NEATENING EDGES, TOP STITCHING AND HEMMING.

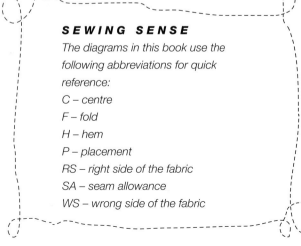

SEWING SENSE
The diagrams in this book use the following abbreviations for quick reference:
C – centre
F – fold
H – hem
P – placement
RS – right side of the fabric
SA – seam allowance
WS – wrong side of the fabric

HAND STITCHING

The most useful hand stitches are basting, hemming, slip stitch and blind hemstitch. Armed with these basics, you are ready to tackle any project.

BASTING

Basting is a way of temporarily holding together two or more layers of fabric with either thread or pins. Pins can be removed more quickly as you sew, but thread will hold the layers more securely.

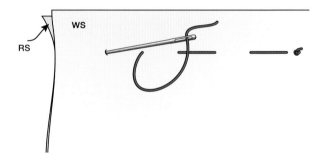

FIGURE 1 BASTING STITCHES ARE TEMPORARY AND WILL BE REMOVED LATER.

When thread basting, use a thread that contrasts with the fabric so it is easy to see and remove later. Make a knot at one end of the thread and start sewing at one end of the seam. Make long running stitches, of even length, through the layers of fabric, along the seam line.

Alternatively, you can also use large basted cross stitches to hold the lining and main fabric together before stitching them permanently.

Once the permanent seam is stitched, remove the basting thread by cutting the knot and pulling the thread out. If a long row of basting stitches has been made, snip the thread at regular intervals along the seam before pulling it out.

To pin baste, insert the pins through the layers of fabric at right angles to the seam so they can be removed as you sew. On small projects, place pins 1–3in (2.5–7.5cm) apart. On large projects, such as curtains, space them every 4–8in (10–15cm).

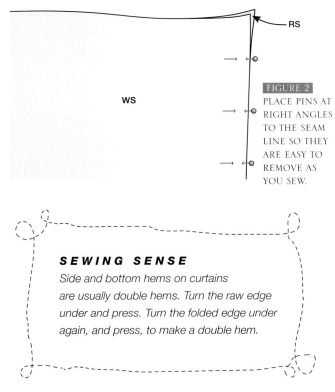

FIGURE 2 PLACE PINS AT RIGHT ANGLES TO THE SEAM LINE SO THEY ARE EASY TO REMOVE AS YOU SEW.

SEWING SENSE

Side and bottom hems on curtains are usually double hems. Turn the raw edge under and press. Turn the folded edge under again, and press, to make a double hem.

TAILOR TACKING

Tailor's tacks are loose stitches sewn on top of each other and are used to mark the position of attachments such as pockets or where two pieces of fabric have to be joined accurately.

1 Using double thread, take the needle down through all the layers of fabric, leaving a 1in (2.5cm) thread tail. Bring the thread back up again close to the thread tail, leaving a loop on the reverse. Repeat twice more, stitching on the spot and leaving loops above and below the fabric.

2 Cut the thread, again leaving a tail. Then carefully cut through the thread loops.

3 Gently pull the fabric layers apart if there are two. Cut the threads between the layers so you have threads left in both layers of fabric.

BAR TACKING

Bar tacks are a series of five to six straight stitches sewn on top of each other to form a definite stop. For instance, if shortening a zipper, cut across at the length required and then bar tack across from one side of the teeth to the other to form a new stop and prevent the zipper pull slipping off.

SLIP STITCH

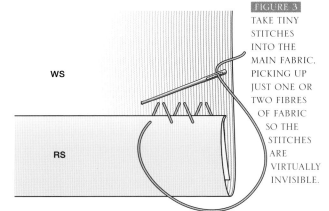

FIGURE 3 TAKE TINY STITCHES INTO THE MAIN FABRIC, PICKING UP JUST ONE OR TWO FIBRES OF FABRIC SO THE STITCHES ARE VIRTUALLY INVISIBLE.

Slip stitch is used to hem lightweight fabrics. Small stitches are taken so that they are virtually invisible on the right side once the hem is stitched.

1 Secure the end of the thread within the folds of the hem.

2 Slip the needle through just one or two fibres of the main fabric and then up through the hem fold at a slight angle to the left. Pull the thread through.

3 Repeat this process to the end of the hem, keeping the stitches and tension even.

EXPERT TIP

TAKE A DOUBLE STITCH ON THE SPOT EVERY 4–5IN (10–12.5CM) ALONG THE HEM TO SECURE THE STITCHING. THEN, IF THE HEM DOES COME UNDONE, ONLY A SMALL SECTION WILL BE AFFECTED.

BLIND HEMMING

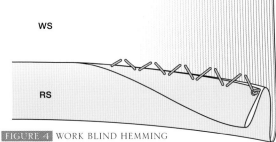

FIGURE 4 WORK BLIND HEMMING IN THE SAME WAY AS SLIP STITCH.

The effects of blind hemming are very similar to slip stitching, but the technique is more suitable for heavier weight fabrics. It prevents an unsightly ridge showing on the right side along the top edge of the hem.

Turn down a little of the folded hem allowance and stitch in the same way as for slip stitching, taking up one or two fibres of main fabric before catching the turned under hem allowance. Repeat along the hem.

HERRINGBONE STITCH

This stitch is particularly usefully for securing side hems. It should not be pulled too tight so it does not pucker the fabric.

1 Work from left to right on the wrong side. Secure the thread end in the folded edge of the hem, bringing the needle out through the hem.

2 Make a small stitch diagonally to the right, inserting the needle horizontally from right to left through the main fabric.

3 Make a second small stitch as before, but this time in the hem fabric. Continue in the same way to the end of the hem.

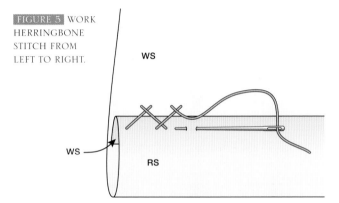

FIGURE 5 WORK HERRINGBONE STITCH FROM LEFT TO RIGHT.

LOCK STITCH

This is a useful stitch for hemming. Because each stitch is locked individually, the hem will not unravel if threads break, which means only a small area needs repairing.

1 Using a small needle, secure the thread end in the folded edge of the hem.

2 Working from right to left, pick up one or two fibres from the main curtain fabric and bring the needle up through the folded hem allowance directly below.

3 Pull the thread until it is almost through and then take the needle, from right to left, under the long loop of thread. Pull through to form a lock stitch.

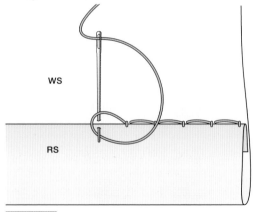

FIGURE 6 MAKE SURE YOU KEEP AN EVEN TENSION WHEN PULLING THE THREAD THROUGH.

4 Continue, making evenly spaced lock stitches, approximately 1in (2.5cm) apart, along the length of the hem.

EXPERT TIP

THE FURTHER APART THE LOCK STITCHES ARE, THE LESS VISIBLE THEY WILL BE ON THE RIGHT SIDE OF THE FABRIC.

LADDER STITCH

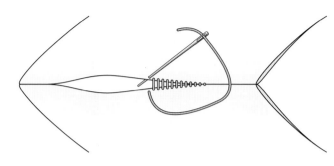

FIGURE 7 PULL THE STITCHES UP AS YOU SEW.

This stitch is used to close relatively short openings, such as those left for turning items like cushion covers and pockets tops through to the right side, or for attaching trims by hand. Like slip stitch and blind hemming, it is almost invisible to see once the stitches are pulled up.

1 First press under the seam allowance on both sides of the opening so that the edges butt perfectly.

2 Secure the thread in the seam allowance and bring the needle to the right side through the fold on one side of the seam.

3 Take a small stitch through the opposite edge of the seam, coming out a short distance along the seam.

4 Now take a small stitch in the first edge of the seam, starting opposite the end of the previous stitch and coming out a short distance along the seam.

5 Continue, gently pulling the thread to close the opening as you sew, until the opening is fully closed.

PRICK STITCH

This stitch is used to insert a zipper by hand or give a decorative top-stitched edge. A row of tiny stitches are visible on the right side so you could use a contrasting colour of thread.

SEWING SENSE

Using chalk pencil, mark a stitch line on the wrong side of the fabric to make sure your stitches stay in a straight row.

1 Secure the thread on the wrong side of the fabric and then bring the needle to the right side. Take a tiny stitch backwards along the seam line, down to the wrong side.

2 Bring the needle up to the right side again approximately ¼in (6mm) along the seam line to the left, ready to make the next back stitch.

FIGURE 8 PRICK STITCH CREATES A LINE OF TINY STITCHES ON THE RIGHT SIDE WITH LONG RUNNING STITCHES ON THE BACK.

GATHERING STITCH

A gathering stitch can be used to gather fabric or ease in a seam. You can gently ease the fullness of a small amount of fabric, for instance on curved hems, so that no visible gathers can be seen on the right side. The smaller the stitches, the smaller the gathers.

1 Secure a double thread on the seam line. To gather, make long running stitches, of even length, along the seam line. You can easily take three or four stitches at a time.To ease stitch, sew within the seam allowance instead.

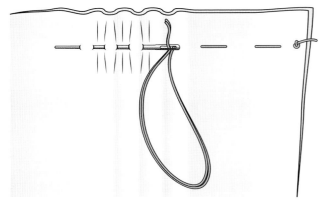

FIGURE 9 TAKE THREE OR FOUR STITCHES AT A TIME TO SEW GATHERING STITCH MORE QUICKLY.

2 When you reach the end of the seam line, pull the thread tails up to gather or ease in the fabric as much as required.

3 To secure the threads and keep the fabric gathered, wrap the thread ends around a vertically placed pin. Alternatively, stitch on the spot to secure thread.

4 Distribute the gathers evenly along the length of fabric or ease the fabric around the curve.

MACHINE STITCHING

The most commonly used machine stitches for making slipcovers are straight stitch and zigzag or overcast stitch. The straight stitch is used to sew regular straight seams and the zigzag or overcast is used to neaten raw edges where the seams will not be visible. Other useful seams are explained on pp.112–115.

> ### SEWING SENSE
> *When sewing, always keep as much of the fabric to the left of your machine as possible. This means that the raw edges of a seam, for example, will run to the right side of the needle in the machine.*

STRAIGHT STITCH

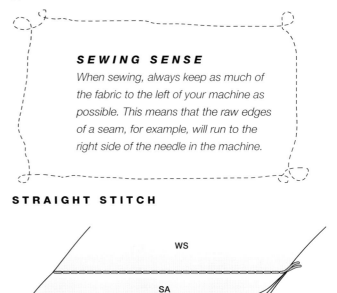

WS

SA

RS

FIGURE 10 RUN THE MACHINE AT A MEDIUM SPEED TO SEW ACCURATELY STRAIGHT ALONG THE SEAM LINE.

Choose a stitch length to suit the fabric being sewn. Lightweight fabrics will need a shorter stitch length of 2.2–2.5; thicker fabrics will need longer stitches of 3–3.5 to prevent the fabric buckling and puckering or the thread breaking. To determine the best length, try straight stitching on remnants of the same fabric, remembering to use the same number of layers and any interfacing, batting, etc. A perfect stitch is perfectly tensioned, with the top thread on the top and the bobbin thread on the underside.

TENSION

With most modern sewing machines, the needle tension is set for general-purpose sewing and doesn't need adjusting for making soft furnishings. If, however, you do find that the needle thread is showing too much on the wrong side of the fabric, then very slightly increase the tension according to instructions in the manual. Test stitch on a remnant of the same fabric and number of layers as being used for project.

GATHERING STITCH

Choose the longest machine stitch and sew within the seam allowance, leaving long thread tails at each end. Secure the thread at one end by wrapping it around a pin. Then pull up the bobbin thread to gather the fabric, moving the gathers along as you go. Continue to gather the fabric until the gathered edge is the same length as the straight edge it is to be attached to. Tie off the thread ends to keep gathers in place.

SEWING SEAMS

FIGURE 11 USE REVERSE STITCH TO STOP THE THREAD UNRAVELLING.

A regular straight seam can be used in many situations including the projects in this book, unless another specific type of seam is recommended. (You will find other seams for specific purposes on pp. 112–115)

Make sure that the thread is secured at the start and finish of a seam to prevent the stitching unravelling. The easiest method is to backstitch or reverse stitch at the beginning and end of the seam.

1 Holding both the bobbin and top threads behind the machine foot, stitch four or five stitches forward along the seam line. Stop and, pressing the reverse button, stitch back over the previous stitches. Now sew forward again to the other end of the seam.

2 Reverse stitch again over the last four or five stitches and then continue forward again to the end of seam.

3 Remove the work from the sewing machine, take the thread tails to the back of the work and trim them close to the fabric.

4 Press the seam, right sides together, to embed the stitches.

SEWING SENSE

On many modern sewing machines.you can press a button to lock the stitch at the beginning and end of the seam instead of reverse stitching.

SEWING SENSE

Always press a seam before stitching over it – once, with right sides together, to embed the stitches; then a second time, with the seam opened out, if you are making a flat seam.

MACHINE BASTING

This has the same function as hand basting, but is achieved by stitching on a machine, set to the longest stitch possible. Stitch without securing the thread at either end (i.e. without reverse stitching) and use a contrasting thread colour so that it is easy to see and remove later.

When you are ready to remove the basting, use scissors or a seam ripper to cut through the stitches at intervals and then pull out the thread tails.

FINISHING SEAMS

Unless seams are encased, they need to be finished or neatened to prevent the fabric fraying during wear. There are different methods for finishing seams, depending on the type of fabric. Whether they are encased or not, you will often need to reduce the bulk of fabric in a seam, or clip or notch a curved seam allowance to allow the fabric to lie flat.

SEWING SENSE

Use pinking shears to quickly neaten lightweight fabrics such as cottons.

Grading is the term for reducing bulk in a seam, which also helps to prevent unsightly ridges showing through on the right side. Press the seam allowances together to one side. Trim the seam allowance closest to the main fabric to a scant ¼in (6mm). Trim the top allowance to ½in (1.3cm).

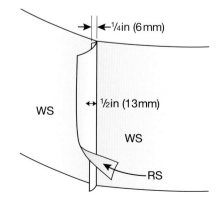

FIGURE 12 GRADE THE SEAM ALLOWANCES TO REDUCE BULK.

Clip across seam allowances at an angle and at regular intervals around an inner curve, so that when the work is turned through, the curved seam allowance will spread out evenly and the seam will not pucker.

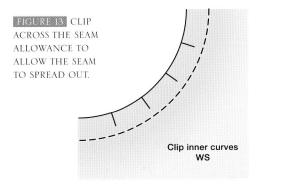

FIGURE 13 CLIP ACROSS THE SEAM ALLOWANCE TO ALLOW THE SEAM TO SPREAD OUT.

Clip inner curves
WS

Notch seams allowances around an outer curve by cutting out little wedge shapes, so that when turned through the allowance will close but not bunch up.

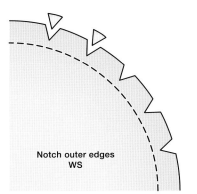

Notch outer edges
WS

FIGURE 14 NOTCH AROUND THE SEAM ALLOWANCE TO ALLOW THE SEAM TO CLOSE UP.

Trimming across a corner will also help to reduce bulk and, when turned through, will produce a crisp right angle. For example, when working on a cushion cover, trim diagonally across the seam allowance on the corners, close to, but not through, the stitching.

SEWING SENSE
Push out the corners using a point turner or, with great care, a pencil or knitting needle.

Zigzagging or **overcasting** is a quick and simple method of neatening raw edges. On lightweight fabrics, neaten both seam allowances together. On medium or heavyweight fabrics, neaten each one separately. Select the zigzag stitch and sew with the right swing of the stitch just off the fabric edge. If an overcast stitch is available, use this with an overcast presser foot.

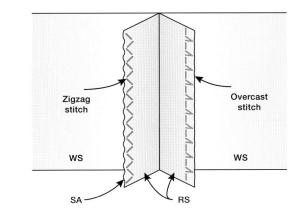

Zigzag stitch

Overcast stitch

WS

WS

SA

RS

FIGURE 15 ZIGZAG OR OVERCAST THE EDGES TO STOP THE FABRIC FRAYING.

EXPERT TIP
ON STRETCH FABRICS, STITCH THE WHOLE ZIGZAG ON THE SEAM ALLOWANCE AND THEN TRIM CLOSE TO THE STITCHING.

Clean finishing is useful for light- to medium-weight fabrics that fray. Press the seam allowance open. Then press under each raw edge and stitch it in place, just through the seam allowance. Press the seam allowances only again.

Hong Kong seams are often used when the reverse side will be visible or for fabrics that fray badly. Press the seam allowances open. Then wrap the raw edges with bias binding or a special stretch tricot tape that folds in half. Pin and stitch the binding or tape in place, with straight stitch on woven fabrics and with zigzag stitch on stretch fabrics.

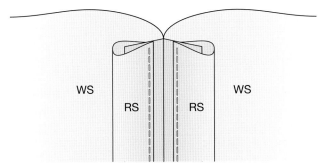

WS

WS

RS

RS

FIGURE 16 BIND THE SEAM ALLOWANCES WITH BIAS BINDING OR TRICOT TAPE.

SEWING SENSE
When pressing, take care that imprints of the seam allowances don't show through to the right side.

TOP STITCH

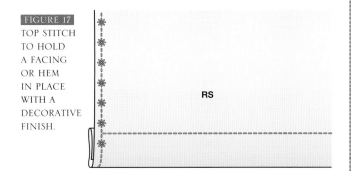

FIGURE 17 TOP STITCH TO HOLD A FACING OR HEM IN PLACE WITH A DECORATIVE FINISH.

This stitching shows on the surface of the fabric. It is used as a decorative finish as well as to hold facings and hems in place. You can choose to use decorative stitches or contrasting thread to make the stitching more of a feature. Although any thread can be used, a top-stitch thread is usually thicker and thus more easily visible. Thicker thread needs to be sewn with a larger-eyed needle and slightly longer stitch length of 3–3.5.

A machine-stitched hem is effectively top-stitched because it will show on the right side. However, if you want the stitching to virtually disappear into the fabric, choose a matching thread. Use a straight stitch and sew close to the top fold of the hem allowance to hold the hem neatly in place.

EDGE STITCH

This is an alternative to top stitching. It also shows on the right side of the fabric, but is sewn closer to the edge of the fabric.

TURNING A DOUBLE HEM

A double hem makes the perfect finish to the side and bottom edges of many projects. Simply turn the raw edge under once, and then again by the same amount. Press, and then stitch it in place by the desired method.

BLIND HEMMING

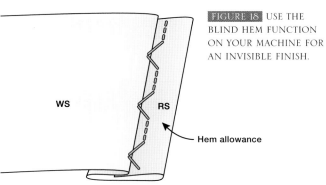

FIGURE 18 USE THE BLIND HEM FUNCTION ON YOUR MACHINE FOR AN INVISIBLE FINISH.

Hem allowance

This very useful machine-stitching technique enables you to hem curtains quickly and almost invisibly!

1 Fold the hem allowance under and neaten the raw edge or tuck it under again. Then fold the hem allowance back under the main fabric to leave just ½–1in (1.25–2.5cm) still showing (see the diagram above).

2 On your machine, select blind hem stitch, which produces a repeat pattern of a few straight stitches followed by one left swing zigzag.

3 Preferably use a blind hem foot, which usually has a thin metal strip protruding below the foot against which you should line up the folded fabric. The straight stitches go into the hem allowance only, with the zigzag swing to the left catching into the folded-back main fabric.

4 Once complete and with the hem allowance hanging properly, the only visible stitch on the right side of fabric is a tiny ladder stitch. However, if the thread matches the fabric closely, this will be virtually invisible.

STITCHING IN THE DITCH

This is a useful technique to master if you want to complete projects by machine and save time on hand stitching. Stitching in the ditch is a way of stitching from the right side in order to keep borders or bindings that are wrapped around to the underside in place on the wrong side.

1 Sew the binding or border to the main fabric, right sides together and with the raw edges matching.

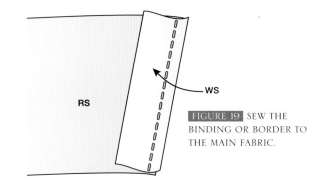

WS

RS

FIGURE 19 SEW THE BINDING OR BORDER TO THE MAIN FABRIC.

2 Trim the seam allowances to a scant ¼in (6mm). If stitching bulky fabric, grade the seam allowances by cutting one to ⅜in (1cm) and the other to ¼in (6mm) in order to reduce bulk.

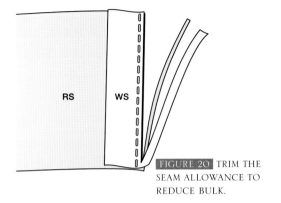

FIGURE 20 TRIM THE SEAM ALLOWANCE TO REDUCE BULK.

3 Press the seam and then press the binding or border open, with the seam allowances towards the raw edge of the binding or border.

4 Fold the binding or border over the raw edges to the wrong side, pinning it in place so that the unattached edge covers the seam line.

5 Working from the right side, place the work under the machine foot so the needle will penetrate the previous seam line. As you stitch in the ditch, pull the seam apart slightly so the new stitches sink into the previous seam line. The underside of the binding or border will also be caught in place by the stitching.

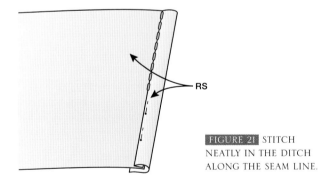

FIGURE 21 STITCH NEATLY IN THE DITCH ALONG THE SEAM LINE.

EXPERT TIP
A stitch-in-the-ditch presser foot, with a very thin metal protrusion below the foot, helps to keep the stitching within the previous seam line.

MITRING CORNERS

A mitred corner gives a crisp professional look to pockets, borders, trims and hems, reducing some of the bulk of the fabric. It is easier to make a symmetrical mitre if the two seam or hem allowances are more less the same width.

1 Using chalk, mark the fold lines on both of the edges to be mitred.

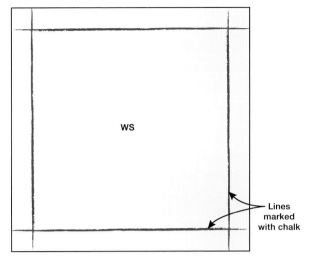

FIGURE 22 MARK THE FOLD LINES ALONG THE EDGES TO BE MITRED.

2 Fold the corner to the wrong side, folding exactly where the marked lines cross and so the folded fabric makes a triangle with two equal sides. Press the fold.

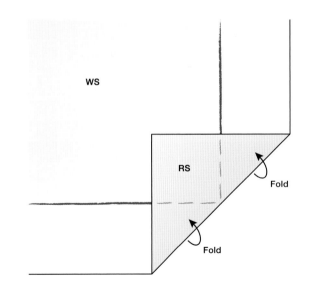

FIGURE 23 FOLD THE CORNER OVER.

3 Unfold the corner and then refold the fabric, right sides together, through the point where the marked lines cross and matching them up along their length. Sew across the seam allowance, starting at the point where the marked lines cross and at right angles to the fold.

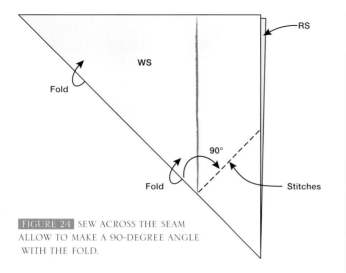

FIGURE 24 SEW ACROSS THE SEAM ALLOW TO MAKE A 90-DEGREE ANGLE WITH THE FOLD.

4 Trim the fabric close to the line of stitching, cutting off the lower triangle. If the fabric frays easily, leave a tiny seam allowance and neaten the raw edge.

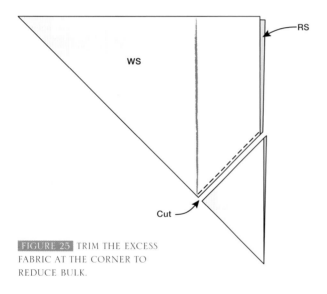

FIGURE 25 TRIM THE EXCESS FABRIC AT THE CORNER TO REDUCE BULK.

5 Press the seam open and then turn the corner out using a point turner.

FIGURE 26 PRESS THE FINISHED MITRED CORNER.

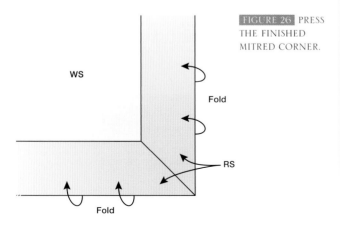

PIVOTING AROUND CORNERS

Sew up to the corner, finishing with the needle in the fabric. Lift the foot and pivot the work, lining up the next line for stitching. Lower the foot and continue stitching.

COVERING BUTTONS

1 To make a fabric covered button cut a circle of fabric one and a half times to twice the diameter of the button form.

2 Sew a running stitch around the outer edge of the fabric and place the button form in the centre on the wrong side.

3 Pull up the thread so that the fabric covers the button form and stitch to hold it in place.

4 Push the raw fabric edges into the cavity of the button form and cover with the backing disk.

5 Push the disk into place with the help of pliers, remembering to protect the button front in the process.

ADDING TRIMS

Attaching trims to soft furnishings can cover seam lines and add attractive detail or a luxurious finish. Trims can be added in the seam, to the reverse of the project so just the beading or fringing is visible or to the surface on the right side. The method of application will depend largely on the type of trim; some have plain tapes which are best concealed, other trims have decorative ribbons or tapes which add to the finished look.

ATTACHING TRIM IN A SEAM

1 Place the trim along the project edge, right sides together, with the plain tape edge of the trim matching the raw edge of the project. Stitch the trim in place down the centre of the tape.

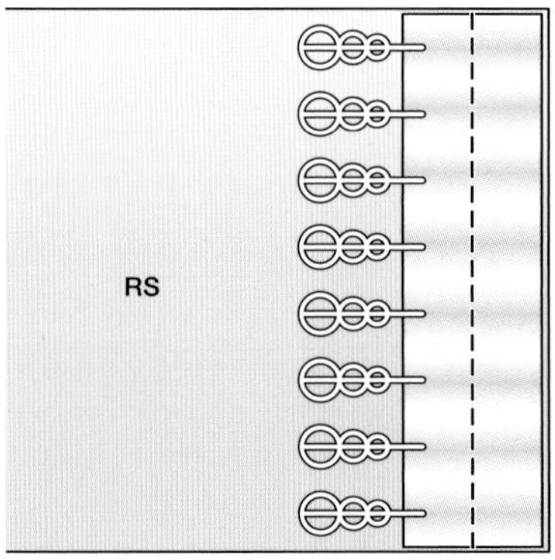

FIGURE 27 ATTACH THE TRIM DOWN THE MIDDLE OF THE TAPE.

2 Place the trimmed fabric on top of the second layer of fabric, right sides together, sandwiching the trim. Using a zipper foot, stitch the seam, sewing as close to the beading as possible. Press.

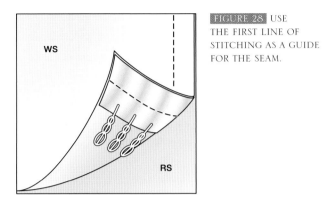

FIGURE 28 USE THE FIRST LINE OF STITCHING AS A GUIDE FOR THE SEAM.

SEWING SENSE

Place the work under the needle with the first stitching holding the tape in place visible so that you can sew easily to the left of the stitching, closer to the actual trim.

3 Turn the fabric to the right side and press. Only the decorative part of the trim will be visible at the seam edge. If desired, top stitch, using a zipper foot to sew close to the edge.

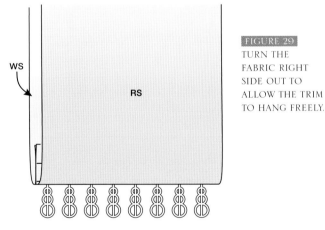

FIGURE 29 TURN THE FABRIC RIGHT SIDE OUT TO ALLOW THE TRIM TO HANG FREELY.

STITCHING TRIM TO THE REVERSE

1 Place the trim along the project edge, right sides together, with the plain tape edge of the trim matching the raw edge of the project. Stitch the trim in place down the centre of the tape. Press the stitching.

2 Fold the project edge to the wrong side so only the trim is visible on the right side. Press and pin in place.

3 Top stitch the hem in place, stitching ³⁄₈in (1cm) from the raw edge.

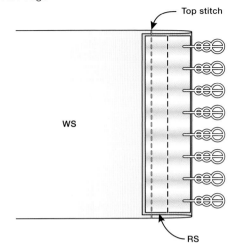

FIGURE 30 HAVING STITCHED THE TRIM TO THE RIGHT SIDE, TURN THE HEM TO THE WRONG SIDE AND TOP STITCH ³⁄₈IN (ICM) FROM THE EDGE.

STITCHING TRIM TO THE SURFACE

You can stitch trim along an edge or at any distance you want from the edge. You can also stitch beading or fringed trim over the top stitching of a hem or so it drops below the bottom edge of the hem.

1 Decide on the best position for the trim. With chalk, mark a guideline for one edge of the trim to ensure it is straight. Pin the trim in place.

2 Select a straight or decorative stitch to machine down both long edges of the trim. For some types of trim, such as beading, it may be necessary to use a zipper foot so you can move the needle position as close as possible to the edge of the trim.

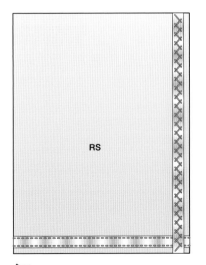

FIGURE 31 ATTACH TRIMS WITH STRAIGHT OR DECORATIVE STITCHES.

EXPERT TIP

STITCH ALONG BOTH LONG EDGES OF TRIM IN THE SAME DIRECTION (FROM TOP TO BOTTOM) TO PREVENT IT FROM BUCKLING OR TWISTING.

FABRIC

A GOOD CHOICE OF FABRIC CAN
MAKE ALL THE DIFFERENCE TO HOW
A PROJECT, AND ULTIMATELY YOUR
ROOM, WILL LOOK. THERE IS AN
ABUNDANCE OF FURNISHING
FABRICS AVAILABLE IN DIFFERENT
TYPES, WEIGHTS AND PATTERNS.
BEFORE MAKING YOUR CHOICE, IT'S
IMPORTANT, THEREFORE, TO MAKE
SURE YOU CONSIDER WHAT THE
FABRIC WILL BE USED FOR,
WHETHER THE COLOUR WILL
ENHANCE THE REST OF THE DÉCOR
AND WHETHER THE TEXTURE OF
THE FABRIC AND THE SIZE OF
ANY PATTERN WILL WORK WELL IN
THE ENVIRONMENT.

Woven fabrics dominate the soft furnishing market. They are woven with warp threads running the length of the fabric and weft (or woof) threads running across the width. They can be plainly woven or have ribbed patterns, twill (diagonal lines on the surface) or a pile or texture giving a velvety surface.

The type of fabric you choose will depend on personal preference and the purpose of the room and the project. You will certainly need to consider:

- the practicalities of the fabric, for example, whether it needs to be hard-wearing or add warmth
- the way the fabric handles and drapes; you may want it to hold pleats crisply, drape softly or gather
- the overall effect of the fabric, whether that is a fresh look or a rich sumptuous feel.

Fabrics for sofa and armchair covers need to be robust and heavyweight, whereas scatter cushion covers can be made from medium-weight silks, satins, faux suede, cotton, chintz, etc. Predominantly natural fibres are best for slipcovers as some synthetics do not retain pleats and ruffles. Good choices for slipcovers include linen, cotton canvas (cotton duck), cotton twill, denim, faux suede, damask, silk taffetas and raw silks.

For advice on choosing and using patterned fabrics, see pp. 120–123.

FOR QUICK, EASY PROJECTS,
CHOOSE FABRICS THAT
ALREADY HAVE LOTS OF
SURFACE DETAIL.

CONSIDER HOW THE
FABRIC WILL DRAPE
ON THE FINISHED
ITEM. SHOULD IT BE
SOFT ENOUGH TO
GATHER OR CRISP
ENOUGH TO HOLD
FIRM PLEATS?

LARGE BOLD
PATTERNS LOOK
GREAT ON BIG PROJECTS
LIKE ARMCHAIRS AND
SOFAS. SMALLER PRINTS
WORK VERY WELL FOR
SCATTER CUSHIONS.

Fabric basics

It is useful to know several terms associated with fabric.

- The **selvages** run along both edges of the length of the fabric. Created as the weft threads turn, they bind the long edges of the fabric and stop it unravelling.
- The **straight**, or **lengthwise**, **grain** refers to the warp threads that run along the length of the fabric parallel to the selvages. The straight grain is usually the most stable.
- The **crossgrain** runs across the fabric width with the weft threads from selvage to selvage and are thus at right angles to the straight grain.
- The **bias** is a 45-degree diagonal line from one selvage to the other. The true bias is found by folding the cut edge to lie on top of a selvage, laying the crossgrain in the same direction as the straight grain. The fabric will stretch most along the true bias.

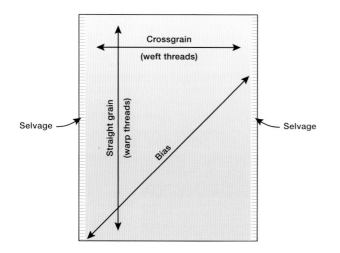

FIGURE 1 FABRIC WILL STRETCH LEAST ALONG THE STRAIGHT GRAIN AND MOST ACROSS THE BIAS.

DEALING WITH SELVAGES

The selvages are usually more tightly bound than the main fabric so it is usually better to cut them off to prevent the seam puckering or twisting. However, sometimes you can match a pattern more easily by seaming the two pieces of fabric together just inside the selvage, using it as a seam allowance. In that case, snip into the selvage every 3–4in (7.5–10cm) so the fabric will lie flat.

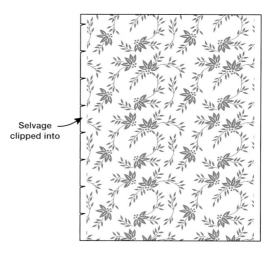

FIGURE 2 SNIP ACROSS THE SELVAGE TO PREVENT SEAMS PUCKERING AND TWISTING.

FABRIC WIDTHS

Soft furnishing fabrics generally come in two main widths: 45/48in (115/122cm) or 54in (138cm). Occasionally you will find cottons that are 60in (150cm) wide.

The width given on the bolt includes the selvages, which may not be useable. If you do cut them off, remember to recalculate the fabric width by the reduced amount.

FABRIC SHRINKAGE

Some fabrics shrink when washed and others are treated with special finishes, to resist dirt and retain the sheen, which would be destroyed by washing. Therefore, for soft furnishings that will need to be washed, such as those in the kitchen, avoid using treated fabrics. If necessary, have them dry-cleaned, although they may still shrink.

EXPERT TIP

VACUUM SOFT FURNISHINGS THOROUGHLY AND REGULARLY. IF POSSIBLE, YOU COULD ALSO TUMBLE THEM IN A TUMBLE DRYER WITH A FEW SHEETS OF FABRIC SOFTENER, WHICH WILL ABSORB THE DIRT.

PATTERN REPEAT

Most furnishing fabrics have a pattern, often repeated down the length of the fabric, either woven in or printed on the front. When making up soft furnishings with more than one width of fabric, you will need to match the pattern across the width. See pp. 122–123 for guidance on how to measure the repeat and match the pattern perfectly.

EXPERT TIP

BEFORE BUYING FABRIC WITH A BOLD PATTERN, CHECK THAT THE PATTERN SITS SQUARELY ACROSS THE FABRIC WIDTH BY UNROLLING IT ON A LARGE CUTTING TABLE IN THE STORE SO THE SELVAGES ARE PARALLEL TO THE TABLE EDGE AND THE FABRIC HANGS OFF THE TABLE. CHECK THE PATTERN IS EVEN ACROSS THE WIDTH OF THE FABRIC AT THE FRONT EDGE OF THE TABLE. VERY SLIGHT INACCURACIES CAN BE HIDDEN IN THE SEAMS, BUT ANYTHING MORE THAN 1½–2IN (3–5CM) SHOULD BE AVOIDED.

STRAIGHTENING FABRIC

Before marking and cutting out the project pieces, first make sure the cut edge is straight by squaring the fabric. The easiest way is to use a set square.

Place one edge of the square down the edge of the selvage so that the other edge of the square sits across the fabric width. Mark across the fabric width. Hopefully the pattern on the fabric runs parallel to the line.

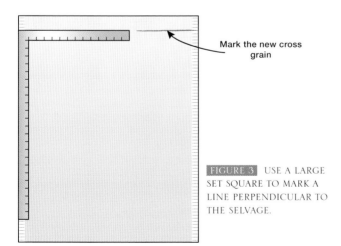

Mark the new cross grain

FIGURE 3 USE A LARGE SET SQUARE TO MARK A LINE PERPENDICULAR TO THE SELVAGE.

If not, line the set square up with the pattern across the width of the fabric, so that the right angle of the square is close to the edge of the selvage. Mark the lengthwise line close to the selvage. Cut along this line and use this cut edge as the new fabric edge.

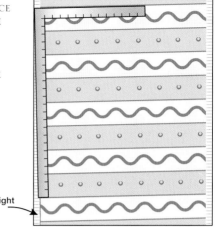

FIGURE 4 PLACE THE SET SQUARE ALONG THE HORIZONTAL PATTERN AND THEN MARK THE NEW STRAIGHT GRAIN.

Mark the new straight grain

EXPERT TIP

ALTHOUGH FABRIC MAY LOOK AS IF IT IS THE SAME WHICHEVER WAY UP YOU LOOK AT IT, SOME FABRICS HAVE SUBTLE SHADING THAT IS ONLY NOTICEABLE WHEN THE PROJECT IS COMPLETE OR THE PATTERN MIGHT BE SLIGHTLY DIFFERENT. SO TO AVOID ANY MISTAKES, ALWAYS CUT ALL THE PIECES IN THE SAME DIRECTION AND MARK THE TOP ON THE BACK OF EACH PANEL TO ENSURE YOU USE THEM ALL THE SAME WAY UP.

FABRIC CALCULATIONS

There are many types of soft furnishing, ranging from single cushion covers to slipcovers for sofas and beds. You can get a good idea of how much fabric you might need for a particular project from the advice given in the projects in this book, but there is no substitute for accurate measurement and good planning. Also remember that you might have to cater for a pattern repeat (see pp. 122–123).

The Projects

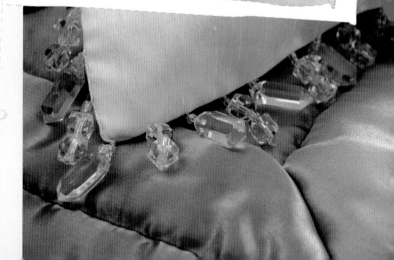

TRIMMING SLIPCOVERS

WORKING WITH PLAIN FABRICS IS EASIER THAN TRYING TO MATCH PATTERNS ON PRINTED FABRIC, BUT IT DOESN'T MEAN PROJECTS NEED TO BE DULL. ADDING TRIM, BEADING OR DECORATIVE STITCHING ISN'T DIFFICULT TO DO — SOME, SUCH AS BEADED TRIMS AND FRINGING, ARE SEWN IN-SEAM, WHILE BRAIDS AND CORDS ARE ATTACHED TO THE FABRIC SURFACE. THEY ALL CREATE TRULY UNIQUE FURNISHINGS.

THE PROJECT ON PP. 34—37 SHOWS YOU HOW A BEADED TRIM ADDS ELEGANT GLAMOUR TO A CUSHION COVER THAT IS SIMPLICITY TO MAKE, WITH NO FIDDLY FASTENINGS.

TOOLS AND EQUIPMENT

✓ Trims of your choice
✓ Basic sewing kit (see p. 8)

TRIMMING CHOICES

- Add beaded or fringed trim with a decorative braid to the hem of a throw for a table, bed or sofa.
- Go wild with ribbon and flat braid to make a very personal cushion cover. You could use treasured scraps and vintage finds to stitch down as a sumptuous lattice on the front of the cover.
- Delve into your button box and add buttons, beads or sequins in the squares of checked fabric or along stripes to dramatically alter the balance of colours on the finished project.

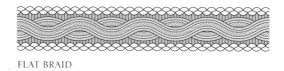

FLAT BRAID

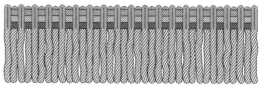

FRINGE

BEADED TRIM

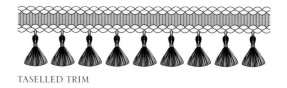

TASELLED TRIM

ATTACHING FLAT TRIMS

Adding a flat trim, in a colour to coordinate with other furnishings and accessories, can really enhance a cushion or pillow cover and turn something plain into a designer original.

1 To attach a flat trim, position it where desired and pin it in place down the centre. For trims over ³⁄₈in (1cm) wide, sew down both long edges. For narrow trims, you can stitch just down the middle. Work with one strip of trim at a time and choose a thread that will match the trim.

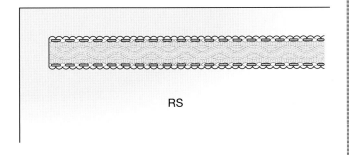

FIGURE 1 SEW ALONG BOTH LONG EDGES OF WIDER TRIMS.

2 Flat trims are usually added before the front and back pieces of the cover are sewn together, so the raw edges of the trim are concealed within the seam allowance. However, you will need to neaten the ends of the trim if you are adding them to an existing cover. Place the trim in position to check the length required and add ³⁄₈in (1 cm) to each end for neatening. Turn this excess to the wrong side and machine or hand stitch the trim in place.

MITRING CORNERS ON FLAT TRIMS

Inevitably, there will be occasions when you want a flat trim to go around a right angle. The neatest way to produce a professional finish is to mitre the trim.

1 Mark the outer placement lines of the trim with chalk. Pin and stitch the trim in place along the line, stitching along both edges up to the adjacent line. Fold the trim back on itself, aligning the edges, and press. Keeping this fold in place, fold the trim again so it runs at right angles to the first line of trim and the outer edge is along the next placement line. Press the mitred fold.

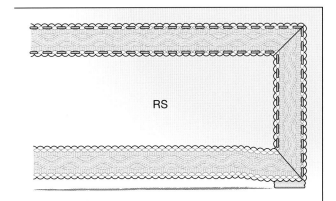

FIGURE 2 FOLD AND PRESS A 45-DEGREE MITRE AT THE CORNER.

2 Undo the second fold so the trim is folded just once, back on itself. Stitch along the diagonal crease through all the layers. Turn the trim back down on the diagonal line of stitching and press. Continue top-stitching the trim in place along both long edges, mitring each corner in turn.

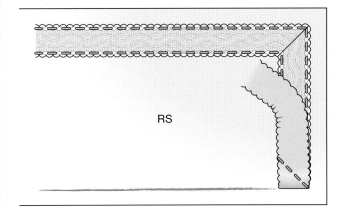

FIGURE 3 STITCH ACROSS THE TRIM, THROUGH ALL THE LAYERS, ON THE DIAGONAL LINE.

EXPERT TIP

FOR BULKY TRIMS, IT MAY BE NECESSARY TO TRIM AWAY THE SEAM ALLOWANCE OF THE DIAGONAL FOLD BEFORE REFOLDING THE TRIM ALONG THE SECOND PLACEMENT LINE.

JOINING ENDS OF FLAT TRIM

If the trim is to go all the way around a cushion front, ends will need to be joined neatly. Simply overlap the trim by 1in (2.5cm), tucking the short raw end of the overlap under. Either machine or hand stitch the tucked end in place.

ATTACHING BEADED TRIM

Beaded trim comes attached to a tape that is either functional

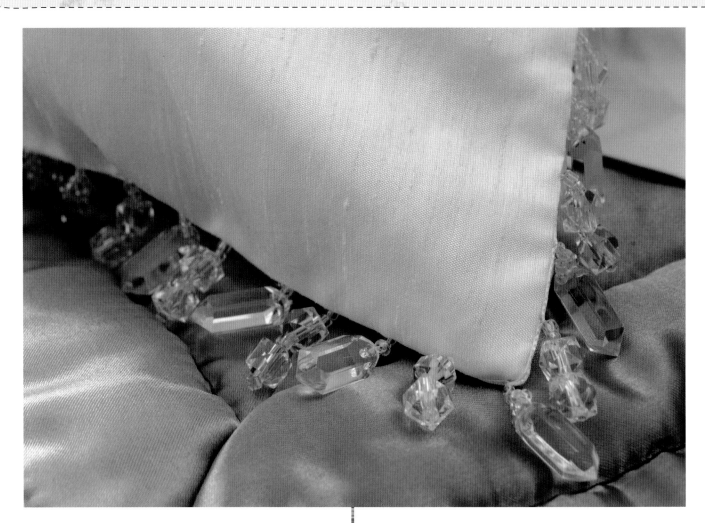

or decorative. While decorative tapes can be sewn to the surface of a project, functional tapes, or flanges, are sewn into seams, allowing the beads or fringe to take centre stage.

If the trim is decorative and used as a surface trim, pick a general-purpose sewing thread in a colour to match the trim. Use a zipper foot on the sewing machine to stitch the trim in position down both long edges.

1 If the trim has a functional flange or you wish to insert it in a seam (for example, on the leading edge of a curtain or as an edging to a cushion cover), pin the trim on the right side of the main fabric, with the straight edge of the flange aligned with the raw edge of the fabric so that only the beads are positioned on the other side of the seam line.

2 Using a zipper foot, stitch the trim in position down the centre of the flange.

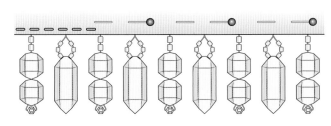

FIGURE 4 USE A ZIPPER FOOT TO STITCH BEADED, OR FRINGED, TRIM IN PLACE.

3 Place the back cover, right sides together over the trimmed front cover and matching the raw edges. With the front cover uppermost, sew through all the layers, stitching to the left of the previous stitches and as close to the beading as possible.

EXPERT TIP
IF THE BEADING IS QUITE LONG AND LIKELY TO FALL INTO THE SEAM LINE, TAPE IT OUT OF THE WAY WITH MASKING TAPE.

JOINING ENDS OF IN-SEAM TRIM

There will be occasions when you need to join a trim on a tape or flange, for example, when trimming around the edge of a cushion cover.

1 To start, pin the trim at right angles to the raw edge of the fabric at the mid-point of one side, rather than at a corner. Then taper the trim around so the straight edge of the tape is parallel and close to the raw edge of the fabric. Pin the trim in place around the project.

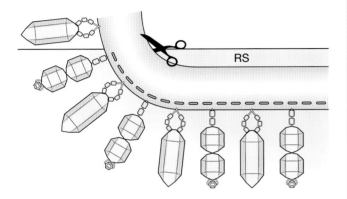

FIGURE 5 ATTACH THE END OF THE TAPE WITHIN THE SEAM ALLOWANCE.

2 At the finish, overlap the tape, tapering the second end off the edge of the fabric. Pin the end in place. If the trim is beaded, remove any beads in the seam allowance by carefully cutting them away or crushing them. Then sew the tape in place, removing the pins.

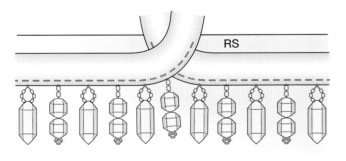

FIGURE 6 OVERLAP THE TAPE AND REMOVE THE BEADS BEFORE STITCHING.

ATTACHING FRINGING

This type of trim is usually attached to a hemmed edge, but is occasionally added as a detail on pockets or cushion covers. Like beaded trims, fringes with decorative tape or edges can be stitched to the surface of a project and those on a flange are inserted within seam allowances in the same way as beaded trims. An alternative is to attach the flange to the back of the hem allowance so just the fringing hangs down. Either top stitch or slip stitch it in place.

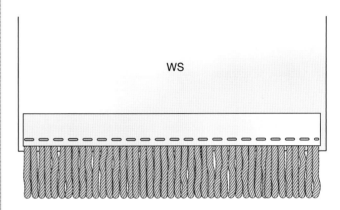

FIGURE 7 SLIP STITCH, OR TOP STITCH, THE FRINGE ALONG THE HEM.

SURFACE FRINGING

Tuck the raw edges under at either end of the trim to neaten and place the fringing in position. If the fringing is to go along a hemline, position it so the fringe drops below the fabric edge. Attach in the same manner as beaded trims.

glitzy CUSHION COVER

RE-COVERING YOUR CUSHIONS IS
PROBABLY THE EASIEST WAY TO UPDATE
YOUR DÉCOR WITH THE MINIMUM OF
FUSS AND COST. THIS ENVELOPE-
BACKED CUSHION COVER CAN BE
MADE IN UNDER AN HOUR AND IS SO
CONVENIENT IF YOU WANT TO REMOVE
THE PAD AND LAUNDER THE COVER.
THE PRE-EMBROIDERED FABRIC SHOWN
HERE GIVES INSTANT DRAMA AND THE
CLASSY GLASS BEADED TRIM MAKES THE
FINISHED CUSHION COVER LOOK A
MILLION DOLLARS!

YOU WILL NEED

✓ Slub silk or similar fabric (see table
below for quantities)
✓ Beaded trim (see table below for length)
✓ 1 reel of matching general-purpose
sewing thread
✓ Zipper foot for sewing machine
✓ Masking tape
✓ Cushion pad (see table below for sizes)
✓ Basic sewing kit (see p. 8)

EXPERT TIP

DON'T ADD EXTRA FABRIC
FOR SEAM ALLOWANCES
TO THE BASIC CUSHION
MEASUREMENTS. THIS WILL
ENSURE THAT YOUR CUSHIONS
LOOK PERMANENTLY PLUMPED.

MATERIALS CALCULATION

For an envelope-backed cushion cover, you need
three pieces of fabric: one front and two back pieces,
which are each about two-thirds of the front piece
so they overlap. The table below gives quantities for
different sized cushions.

TECHNICAL KNOW-HOW

Attaching beaded trim (p. 32)
Top stitching (p. 20)
Grading seam allowances (p. 18)

FINISHED SIZE	NUMBER OF PIECES	FABRIC	PAD	TRIM
14in (35cm) square	1 2	14in (35cm) square 9 x 14in (23 x 35cm) square	14in (35cm) square	1 ¾ yd (1.6m)
16in (40cm) square	1 2	16in (40cm) square 12 x 16in (30 x 40cm) square	16in (40cm) square	2yd (1.7m)
18in (46cm) square	1 2	18in (46cm) square 12 x 18in (30 x 36cm) square	18in (46cm) square	2⅛yd (2m)
20in (50cm) square	1 2	20in (50cm) square 14 x 20in (35 x 50cm) square	20in (50cm) square	2⅜yd (2.2m)

PREPARING THE FABRIC PANELS

1 Cut one piece of fabric for the front of the cushion cover and two pieces for the back as economically as you can from the fabric. See the table on p. 34 for the sizes of fabric pieces needed for four different sizes of cushion cover. Remember to match the pattern as necessary or position it on the pieces to best effect.

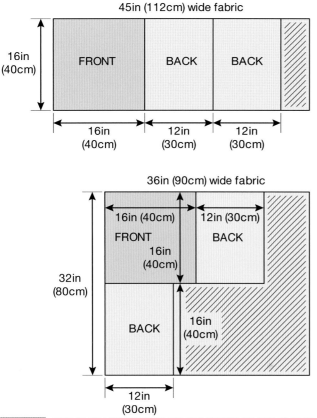

FIGURE 1   CUT AS MANY PIECES FROM THE WIDTH OF THE FABRIC AS YOU CAN.

EXPERT TIP

IF MAKING QUITE A FEW CUSHIONS, MAKE CARDBOARD TEMPLATES FOR THE FRONT AND BACK PIECES. USE THESE TO MEASURE AND MARK ALL THE NECESSARY PIECES.

2 Neaten one long edge on each back piece by turning under ½in (1.3cm) twice to form a double hem. Top stitch it in place. Press and set the pieces to one side.

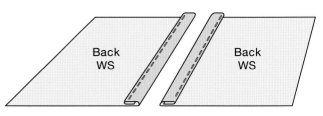

FIGURE 2   TURN UNDER A HEM ON EACH OF THE EDGES ON THE BACK PIECES THAT WILL OVERLAP.

ATTACHING THE BEADED TRIM

1 Pin the beaded trim to the right side of the front piece of fabric, starting at the edge of the fabric in the middle of one side and then matching the straight edge of the tape to the raw edge of the fabric, so that only the beads are positioned on the other side of the seam line. At the corners, clip into the tape so it turns around 90 degrees easily.

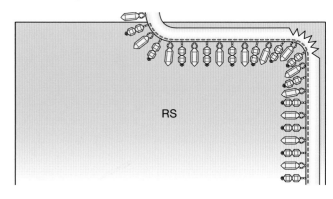

FIGURE 3   CLIP THE TAPE AT THE CORNERS SO IT WILL GO AROUND THEM EASILY.

2 Where the ends of the trim meet at the start point, overlap the trim, taking the second end over the edge of the fabric again (see p. 33).

3 Remove the beads within the seam allowance. Then, using a zipper foot, sew the trim in place.

FINISHING THE CUSHION COVER

1 With right sides together, pin the back pieces onto the front, with the hemmed edges overlapping in the centre and the outer raw edges aligned. Insert the pins at right angles to the raw edges so they can be removed easily as you sew.

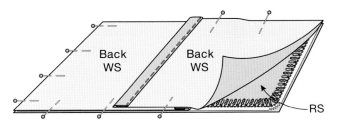

FIGURE 4 PIN THE PIECES RIGHT SIDES TOGETHER, OVERLAPPING THE HEMMED EDGES.

EXPERT TIP

IF THE BEADS GET IN THE WAY, TEMPORARILY TAPE THEM DOWN WITH MASKING TAPE.

2 Turn the cushion cover over and work with the front uppermost. Stitch all around the outside edges, taking a ⅝in (1.5cm) seam allowance and stitching to the left of the previous stitching. Trim the corners diagonally and press.

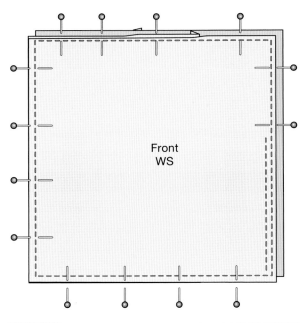

FIGURE 5 STITCH THE FRONT AND BACK PIECES TOGETHER, SANDWICHING THE TRIM IN THE SEAM.

3 Turn the cushion cover through the opening in the centre back, using a point turner to ease out the corners. Press again. Stuff the cover with the cushion pad.

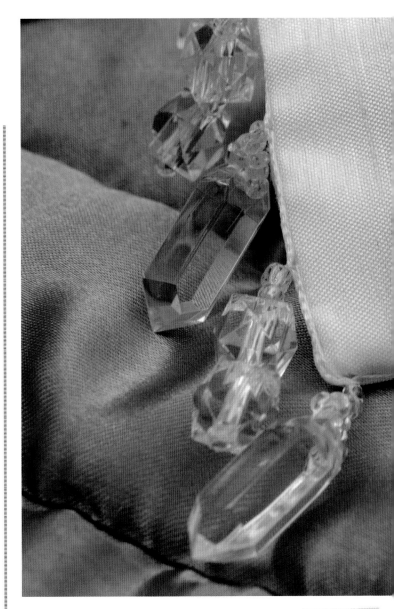

MORE DESIGN IDEAS

• Use two different fabrics for the front panel. Stitch two pieces together to make the square, placing the seam horizontally, vertically or even diagonally.
• Instead of sewing in beaded trim, add decorative trim across the front of the cover before stitching it to the back.
• Adapt the instructions to make oblong and even round envelope-backed cushion covers.
• Mark out guidelines on the front cover and add decorative stitches in colourful threads before making up the cover.

MAKING BUTTONS, TIES AND STRAP FASTENINGS

BUTTONS, TIES AND STRAPS FASTEN AND HOLD SLIPCOVERS IN PLACE. THEY ALSO PROVIDE THE PERFECT OPPORTUNITY TO ADD DECORATIVE DETAIL. THEY CAN BE MADE FROM THE SAME FABRIC AS THE MAIN PROJECT OR IN A LOVELY CONTRAST FABRIC TO GIVE AN ACCENT OF COLOUR, A MIX OF PATTERNS OR ANOTHER TEXTURE.

THE KITCHEN CHAIR CUSHION ON PP. 42—45 MAKES GOOD USE OF BUTTONS AND TIES TO GIVE A SOFT AND COMFORTABLE PADDED SEAT.

TOOLS AND EQUIPMENT
✓ Fusible interfacing
✓ Self-covered buttons
✓ String or cord
✓ Basic sewing kit (see p. 8)

BUTTON AND TIE CHOICES
- Choose a fabric in a colour featured in the main project fabric so you can make a statement but be sure that the combination works well.
- Try embroidering a simple flower shape onto the fabric before cutting it out and using it to cover buttons. With a little patience, you can also encrust buttons with beads by sewing them onto the fabric in advance.
- Add contrast ties and buttons to a neutral colour scheme so you can coordinate with other accessories.

SEWING SENSE
If working with patterned fabric, choose a part of the design for the buttons or ties to show the fabric to the best advantage. For example, running stripes along the length of ties or centring a flower motif on a button adds a professional touch.

COVERING BUTTONS

Covering buttons in your own fabric allows you to add a matching or contrasting trim that perfectly suits the furnishing. The button forms are available in silver metal or white plastic in a variety of sizes and the method for covering them is very simple.

EXPERT TIP
IF WORKING WITH LOOSELY WOVEN OR BULKY FABRIC FOR THE MAIN PROJECT, WHICH WILL BE DIFFICULT TO GATHER AND SECURE UNDER THE BUTTON BACK, CHOOSE A LIGHTER WEIGHT COTTON IN A SIMILAR COLOUR TO COVER THE BUTTONS INSTEAD.

1 Apply fusible interfacing to the wrong side of the fabric for the buttons. Then cut circles of the fabric using the template in the manufacturer's instructions or one and a half to twice the diameter of the button.

2 Hand sew running stitches around the outside of the fabric circle. Then, with the needle still attached, place the button on the wrong side of the fabric.

EXPERT TIP
WHEN USING FINE TRANSPARENT FABRIC, FIRST COVER THE BUTTON WITH A LIGHTWEIGHT WOVEN INTERFACING.

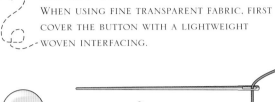

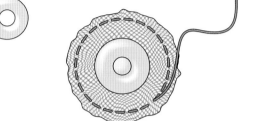

FIGURE 1   SEW SMALL RUNNING STITCHES AROUND THE EDGE OF THE FABRIC.

3 Pull up the stitches and the edges of the fabric around the button. Stitch on the spot to secure the gathering and trim the thread ends.

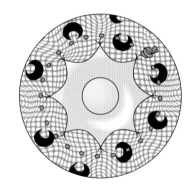

FIGURE 2   GATHER THE FABRIC AROUND THE BUTTON.

4 Clip the back of the button over the gathered fabric, covering the raw edges, and push it firmly into place.

MAKING STRAPS AND TIES

Straps and ties secure chair cushions and covers in place. Straps are wider and can be fastened with buttons or poppers, whereas ties tend to be narrow and come in pairs to be tied together. Either can be made from braid or ribbon as well as from the main project or a contrast fabric.

EXPERT TIP

TIES CUT ON THE BIAS OF THE FABRIC HAVE MORE STRETCH AND FOLD AROUND CURVES MORE EASILY. THOSE CUT ON THE STRAIGHT GRAIN ARE MORE STABLE.

1 To make ties or straps, first cut out a long rectangle of fabric to the length and width required. Ties for chair cushions should be at least 13in (33cm) long and 1½in (4cm) wide.

SEWING SENSE

To add more stability to straps, back the fabric with lightweight interfacing.

2 Fold the fabric in half lengthways, with right sides together, and machine stitch the long edge taking a ¼in (6mm) seam. Turn through to the right side, twisting the fabric so the seam is at the centre back. Alternatively, if you are making very long ties, stitch across one short end, then along the long edge, leaving a 4in (10cm) opening in the seam. Then stitch to the end and then across the other short end. Trim the seam allowances and corners and turn through the opening. Slip stitch the opening closed. Press.

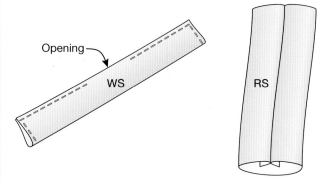

Opening

WS

RS

FIGURE 3 CHOOSE THE APPROPRIATE SEAM FOR THE LENGTH OF THE TIE.

EXPERT TIP

USE A LENGTH OF STRING OR CORD, ABOUT 5IN (13CM) LONGER THAN THE FABRIC, TO HELP YOU TURN A STRAP OR TIE EASILY. FOLD THE FABRIC IN HALF LENGTHWAYS, RIGHT SIDES TOGETHER, WITH THE CORD INSIDE THE FOLD. SECURE THE CORD AT ONE END WITH A STITCH OR TWO BEFORE STITCHING THE SEAM, WITHOUT CATCHING THE CORD. TO TURN THROUGH, PULL ON THE CORD. CUT OFF THE CORD, READY TO USE AGAIN.

3 Tuck the two raw ends to the inside and press. Stitch one end closed. Attach the other end to the project either by inserting it into the seam of the slip cover or by stitching it to the surface.

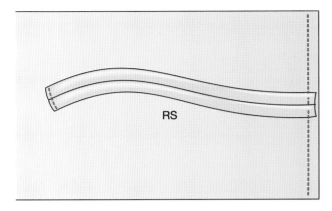

FIGURE 4 ATTACH THE TIE TO THE RIGHT SIDE OF THE FABRIC BEFORE STITCHING IT INTO THE SEAM.

4 To secure a strap or tie to the right side of fabric, pin about 1½in (4cm) of its length onto the fabric. Stitching ¼in (6mm) from the edge, sew across the short end, encasing the tucked-in raw edges. Turn and continue sewing along the edge to within ¼in (6 mm) of the edge of the project. Turn and continue across the top, and then along the final side, to make a box shape. To further secure the strap or tie, stitch a cross inside the box.

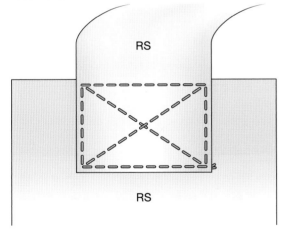

FIGURE 5 STITCH A CROSSED BOX TO SECURE THE END OF A STRAP OR TIE.

MAKING ROULEAU LOOPS

Rouleau loops, made from thin spaghetti straps cut from bias strips of fabric, are most often seen on garments, but the same technique can be adapted for soft furnishings. They can be used as a fastening with ball buttons or can create very effective surface decoration.

1 Cut a bias strip of fabric about ¾in (2cm) wide by the length required. If you need to join strips to get the length you need, see pp. 59–60.

2 Fold the strip in half lengthways, with right sides together, and stitch the seam as in step 2 on p. 40 above. Leave the seam allowances on, which will fill the tube, making it more rounded. Turn the strip through to the right side using string or cord, as described in the expert tip at the bottom of p. 40.

3 Determine the length needed for the loops by measuring the diameter of the button and adding 1¼in (3cm) for the seam allowances at each end. Cut the strip into the required lengths.

4 Fold the loops in half and pin them to the right side of the project fabric, matching the raw edges. When all the loops are pinned, stitch along the seam line, securing them in place.

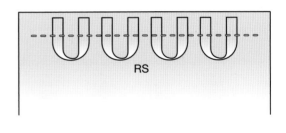

FIGURE 6 STITCH ACROSS ALL THE LOOPS.

5 Complete the project, by either simply turning the seam allowance to the inside so that the loops stand proud of the edge or incorporating them into a seam before turning the fabric through.

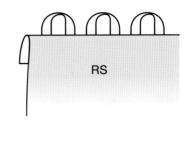

FIGURE 7 TURN THE FABRIC THROUGH SO THE LOOPS STAND PROUD OF THE EDGE.

kitsch
KITCHEN CHAIR CUSHION

TAKE THE WEIGHT OFF YOUR FEET IN COMFORT BY MAKING A SET OF DEEP PADDED AND BUTTONED CUSHIONS FOR THE KITCHEN. THIS DESIGN HAS SELF-COVERED BUTTONS AND TIES TO SECURE IT TO THE CHAIR, AND OOZES RETRO-CHIC WITH ITS BOLD RED AND WHITE PATTERN. INSTEAD OF THE FIVE BUTTON POSITIONS SHOWN HERE, YOU COULD USE FOUR OR JUST ONE ON A CUSHION OF THIS SIZE.

YOU WILL NEED
(per cushion)

✓ ¾yd (60cm) medium-weight soft furnishing fabric
✓ Dressmaker's pattern or brown parcel paper
✓ 1 reel of matching general-purpose sewing thread
✓ 10oz (300g) polyester wadding
✓ 8–10 self-cover buttons (2 for each button position)
✓ Button twist or strong thread
✓ Large needle or bodkin
✓ Basic sewing kit (see p. 8)
Note: The amount of fabric and wadding will vary according to the size and shape of the seat.

TECHNICAL KNOW-HOW
Covering buttons (see p. 39)

PREPARING THE PATTERN

1 Placing a piece of pattern paper on the seat of the chair, draw around the shape, following the outline at the front and up to the struts at the back. Neaten up the shape on the paper, making sure it is symmetrical. Then add a ⅝in (1.5cm) seam allowance all around the outer edge. Determine where you want buttons to be placed and mark their positions with crosses on the pattern. The positioning is personal preference, but looks best if the buttons are symmetrical. For example, with four, each button could be positioned about 2–3in (5–7.5cm) from the corners; add a fifth in the centre; or place just one button in the centre.

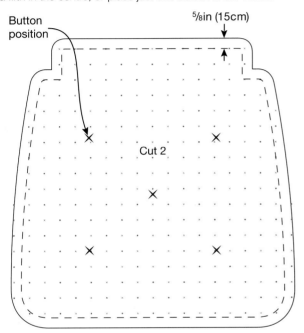

FIGURE 1 ADD THE SEAM ALLOWANCE AND BUTTON POSITIONS TO THE TEMPLATE.

2 Measure the outside circumference of the seat to calculate the length of the gusset. Add 1¼in (3cm) for seam allowances.

CUTTING THE FABRIC

1 Cut two pieces of fabric for the top and bottom of the cushion. Using tailor tacks, chalk or wash-away marker, transfer the button positions to the right side of both pieces of fabric.

2 Cut a rectangle of fabric for the gusset: it should be the length plus seam allowances by 2¾in (7cm) for the width (which includes seam allowances).

3 Cut a length of fabric 3 x 40in (8cm x 1m) ready to make all the ties for the cushion.

MAKING UP THE CUSHION

1 Cut the fabric for the ties in half, making two 20in (50cm) strips. Fold one strip of fabric lengthways, with right sides together and aligning the raw edges. Sew across one end, along the long raw edge and then across the other end, securing the threads with reverse stitches. Cut the strip in half to create two ties. Turn the ties through and press flat. Repeat with the other strip. Put the ties to one side.

2 Stitch the gusset into a circle by sewing the two short ends together, with right sides together and a ⅝in (1.5cm) seam allowance. Press the seam open.

3 With right sides facing, pin the gusset around the raw edges of the fabric for the top of the cushion. Make sure you match up the raw edges and pin the seam on the gusset to the centre of the back edge of the top panel. Snip into the seam allowance of the gusset around the corners to allow it to lie flat. Stitch the pieces together, reinforcing the corners with a second row of stitching next to the first. Trim and press the seam open.

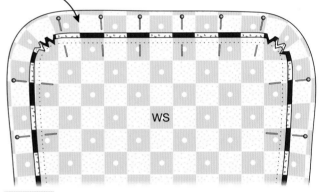

FIGURE 2 SNIP INTO THE SEAM ALLOWANCE AROUND THE FRONT AND BACK CORNERS.

4 Working on the right side of the cushion back and matching the raw edges, pin a pair of ties to each back corner of the cushion close to where the outer back struts of the chair will be. Baste the ties in place.

FIGURE 3 BASTE THE TIES IN POSITION ON THE BACK CORNERS OF THE CUSHION.

5 Match up the back cushion panel with the gusset as for the top panel and pin them together, snipping into the seam allowance as before. Stitch them together, leaving an opening of about 6in (15cm) across the centre back to allow turning and filling the cushion. Sew a second row of stitching next to the first to strengthen the cushion. Trim the seam allowances to about ¼in (6mm) and turn through.

6 Fill the cushion evenly with polyester wadding and then slip stitch the opening closed. Use double thread and small stitches for a secure finish.

ATTACHING THE BUTTONS

1 Cover ten buttons with scraps of the cushion fabric (see p. 39 for covering buttons).

2 Thread a long needle or bodkin with a double length of button twist. Thread the needle through one button, leaving a tail of about 4in (10cm). Tie a double knot with the tail and needle thread to secure the button onto the thread.

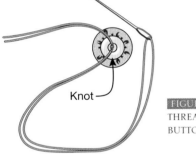

Knot

FIGURE 4 KNOT THE THREAD AROUND THE BUTTON TO SECURE IT.

3 Take the needle down through a position mark on the top of the cushion to the corresponding mark on the bottom. Then slide the needle through a second button.

4 Take the needle back up to the top of the cushion, through the same marks, and pull the thread tight. Tie a double knot in the two thread tails. Cut off the thread tails. Repeat, to secure the remaining buttons.

FIGURE 5 PULL THE THREAD TIGHT SO THAT THE BUTTONS INDENT THE CUSHION.

5 Place the cushion on the seat of the chair and tie it securely to the back struts.

MAKING A SIMILAR CUSHION WITHOUT A GUSSET

1 Make a paper pattern for the top and bottom of the cushion as before, but simplify the corners by giving them 90-degree angles. Add about 2in (5cm) on all sides.

2 Attach the ties as before, but to the cushion top. With right sides together, sew the cushion top to the bottom, trapping the ties in the back seam and leaving a 6in (15cm) opening.

3 Before turning the cushion through, press the seams open. Then, taking each corner in turn, refold it so the adjacent seams sit one on top of the other. Sew across the corner at 90 degrees to the seam, about 1½–2in (4–5cm) from the point of the corner. When turned through, this provides depth to the cushion without adding a gusset. The further from the corner you sew, the deeper the cushion will be.

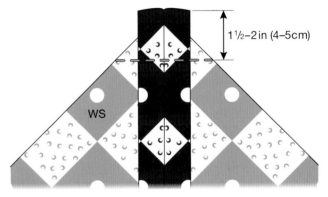

1½–2in (4–5cm)

WS

FIGURE 6 SEW ACROSS THE CORNER TO ADD MORE DEPTH TO THE CUSHION.

4 Finish the cushion as before.

MORE DESIGN IDEAS

• Add piping to the gusset seams to define the edges of the cushion, covering piping cord (see p. 79) with the cushion fabric or a contrasting colour, or choosing coordinating flanged cord.

• Use ribbons as ties, choosing a colour to complement the cover fabric. Attach them into the seam before stitching the back and front of the cover together.

• Attach very thin ties to the cushion and decorate them by tying a large wooden bead to each loose end.

EMBELLISHING WITH APPLIQUÉ

AN APPLIQUÉ IS A MOTIF APPLIED TO ANOTHER FABRIC. THESE MOTIFS ADD ANOTHER DIMENSION TO A PROJECT AND CAN BE USED TO HIGHLIGHT AN AREA, CREATE CONTRAST OR SIMPLY ADD SURFACE DETAIL.

DIFFERENT METHODS GIVE VARIOUS RESULTS. HERE THE MOST COMMONLY USED ARE EXPLAINED: SEWING MOTIFS TO THE RIGHT SIDE OF THE MAIN FABRIC, RAW EDGE APPLIQUÉ AND CREATING REVERSE APPLIQUÉ, WHICH IS APPLIED FROM BELOW.

THE DIRECTOR'S CHAIR ON PP. 52–57 SHOWS HOW QUICKLY AND EASILY YOU CAN CREATE A FUNKY NEW LOOK, WHILE THE FLAT PANELS ARE IDEAL TO FLAUNT YOUR APPLIQUÉ SKILLS. AS WELL AS FLAT MOTIFS, YOU COULD EXPERIMENT WITH THREE-DIMENSIONAL EFFECTS.

APPLIQUÉ CHOICES

- Any fabric that has the same wash and care requirements as the main fabric can be used for appliqué. The most suitable are fabrics that do not ravel easily and include cottons, polyester/cottons, fleece and stretch knits.
- Cut simple shapes such as flowers and leaves from the main fabric and apply them as three-dimensional appliqué on top of the same motifs on the chair back fabric to give them a beautifully textured effect.
- Embroider the appliqué shapes with decorative threads and beads before applying them to the fabric.

TOOLS AND EQUIPMENT

- ✓ Double-sided fusible web or temporary craft adhesive (for bonding)
- ✓ Fusible interfacing (for reverse appliqué)
- ✓ Matching or contrasting thread for appliqué
- ✓ Sharp embroidery scissors
- ✓ Basic sewing kit (see p. 8)

BONDING APPLIQUÉ IN PLACE

You can bond appliqué to fabric without any other method of securing it, or to simply hold a motif in place prior to stitching it down. Although the bonding is relatively secure, it can work loose on items that receive heavy wear or frequent washing, and stitching is advised. Use double-sided fusible web with a paper backing or temporary craft adhesive on the reverse of the appliqué shape.

SEWING SENSE

It is always a good idea to bond appliqué to the main fabric first, even if you are going to stitch it in place. This will stop it moving while you are stitching – especially around small areas of a motif.

USING FUSIBLE WEB

1 Cut out a simple square or rectangle from the appliqué fabric, allowing at least ½in (1.3cm) around the appliqué shape. Iron fusible webbing onto the wrong side of the fabric, following the manufacturer's instructions. Leave to cool completely and then carefully cut around the appliqué shape.

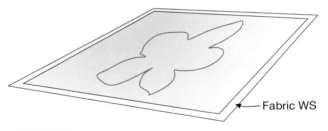

— Fabric WS

FIGURE 1 IRON THE FUSIBLE WEB TO THE WRONG SIDE OF THE APPLIQUÉ FABRIC.

EXPERT TIP

IF YOU ARE CREATING YOUR OWN MOTIF, DRAW THE DESIGN ON THE PAPER BACKING OF THE FUSIBLE WEB. FUSE THE APPLIQUÉ FABRIC TO THE FUSIBLE WEB AND THEN CUT THE SHAPE OUT.

2 Peel off the paper backing and stick the motif firmly in position onto the main fabric using a hot iron and press cloth.

USING CRAFT ADHESIVE

1 Cut out the motif from the appliqué fabric and place it right side down on a large sheet of paper. Working in a well-ventilated room, or outside, lightly spray the adhesive onto the fabric.

2 While still tacky, position the motif on the right side of the main fabric and press it in place.

CREATING STANDARD SATIN-STITCHED APPLIQUÉ

Appliqué is stitched in place to secure it firmly, no matter what wash and wear it will have, and to prevent the edges ravelling. The most common stitch used is machine satin stitch, which is a very close zigzag stitch.

1 The stitch width setting controls the width of the satin stitch and the length setting controls how close the stitches are together. Start by setting the stitch width at 3 and the length at 0.5, and then adjust as necessary.

2 Position the appliqué and main fabric under the machine needle so that the left swing of the needle stitches into the appliqué and the right swing stitches into the main fabric, effectively covering the raw edge of the motif and securing it to the main fabric. Stitch around the shape, following the guidance below for handling any curves and corners.

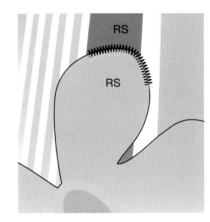

FIGURE 2 MAKE SURE THE LEFT SWING OF THE NEEDLE STITCHES INTO THE APPLIQUÉ AND THE RIGHT SWING INTO THE MAIN FABRIC.

3 Continue until you have stitched all around the shape. Take the thread ends to the rear and work them into the back of the work. Carefully press the appliqué.

EXPERT TIP

ALWAYS TEST STITCHING ON THE SAME FABRIC AND NUMBER OF LAYERS TO CHECK THAT THE STITCHES COVER THE RAW EDGES PROPERLY AND ARE CLOSE ENOUGH TOGETHER.

HANDLING CURVES AND CORNERS

Stitching neatly around curves and corners may look tricky, but following a few simple guidelines will make the process easier. Start with the appliquéd fabric to the left of the needle.

STITCHING AROUND OUTER CURVES

1 Stitch slowly around the curve so that the lines of stitches sit at right angles to the edge of the shape. As you progress and this becomes less possible, stop stitching, with the needle down in the main fabric on a right swing.

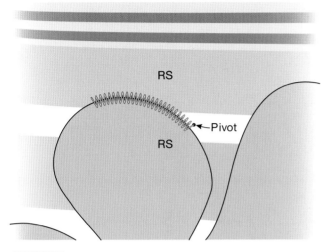

FIGURE 3 LEAVE THE NEEDLE IN THE MAIN FABRIC BEFORE PIVOTING THE FABRIC TO STITCH AROUND OUTER CURVES.

2 Raise the presser foot, pivot the fabric slightly and lower the foot again. Continue stitching, pivoting regularly to stitch smoothly around the curved area.

STITCHING AROUND INNER CURVES

1 Start as for outer curves. When you need to adjust the stitching line, stop stitching, with the needle down in the appliqué fabric on a left swing.

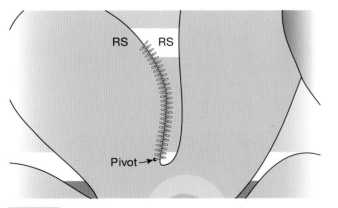

FIGURE 4 LEAVE THE NEEDLE IN THE APPLIQUÉ FABRIC BEFORE PIVOTING THE FABRIC TO TAKE THE STITCHING AROUND INNER CURVES.

2 Raise the presser foot and pivot the fabric as before. Continue stitching making regular adjustments.

STITCHING AN OPEN CORNER

1 On a shape with a square corner, stitch to the corner and stop with the needle down in the left-hand position, i.e. in the appliqué fabric.

2 Raise the presser foot and pivot the fabric to line up the next edge of appliqué. Lower the foot and continue stitching, leaving a neat square gap at the corner.

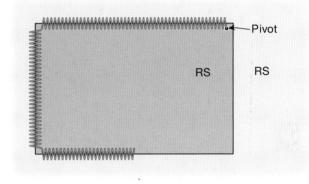

FIGURE 5 PIVOT THE FABRIC WITH THE NEEDLE IN THE LEFT-HAND POSITION TO LEAVE AN OPEN CORNER.

STITCHING A CLOSED CORNER

1 To give a different finish to a square corner, stitch to the corner, but stop with the needle down in the right-hand position, i.e. in the main fabric.

2 Raise the presser foot and pivot the fabric to line up the next edge of appliqué. Lower the foot and continue, stitching over the top of the last few stitches.

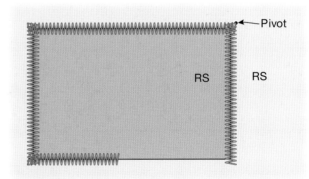

FIGURE 6 PIVOT THE FABRIC WITH THE NEEDLE IN THE RIGHT-HAND POSITION TO STITCH A CLOSED CORNER.

OVERLAPPING EDGES

When appliqué shapes overlap, stitch the lower pieces first, stopping a scant ⅛in (3mm) from the overlapping piece so that the satin stitching will not overlap. This will reduce bulk and prevent the machine from jamming, as some sewing machines really do not like stitching over the top of dense stitching. Satin stitch around the uppermost motif in the usual way.

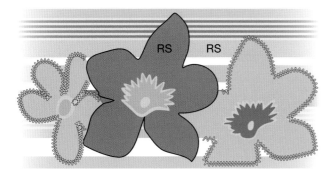

FIGURE 7 STITCH AROUND THE PARTS OF THE LOWER MOTIFS THAT WILL NOT LIE UNDER THE TOP MOTIFS.

LEAVING RAW EDGES

As the name suggests, the edges on raw edge appliqué are left raw to ravel. This method of appliqué is therefore quick and easy to achieve. Good fabrics to use are those that ravel easily, such as hemp and wool, or those that are not too tightly woven and can have threads removed, like cotton and calico.

EXPERT TIP

IF EDGES ARE TO BE PURPOSELY FRAYED OR FRINGED (BY REMOVING THREADS FROM EDGE), WORK WITH STRAIGHT EDGES AND SIMPLE SHAPES SUCH AS SQUARES AND RECTANGLES.

1 Cut out the appliqué fabric, cutting it about ⅜in (1cm) larger than finished shape.

2 Using straight stitch, stitch around the shape ⅜in (1cm) from the edge.

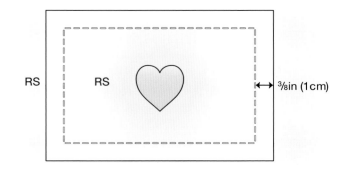

FIGURE 8 STITCH ⅜IN (1CM) IN FROM THE EDGE AROUND THE SHAPE.

3 Apply fusible web within the stitched area only and then fuse the motif in place on the main fabric.

4 Straight stitch, or use a decorative machine stitch, to secure the motif, stitching ⅛in (3mm) inside the previous straight stitching and allowing the outer ⅜in (1cm) edge to remain loose from the main fabric.

FIGURE 9 ADD ANOTHER LINE OF STITCHING INSIDE THE FIRST.

5 Either draw out threads from around the edges of the appliqué fabric, gently pulling them out until a fringe is achieved, or wash and tumble dry the item to rough up the raw edges.

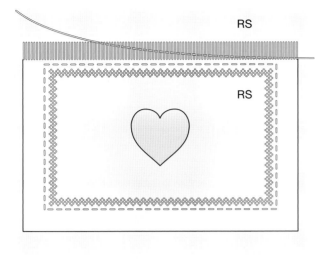

FIGURE 10 WITHDRAW THREADS TO CREATE AN ATTRACTIVE FRINGE AROUND THE APPLIQUÉ.

CREATING REVERSE APPLIQUE

Reverse appliqué is applied to the back of the main fabric, which is then cut out to shape before satin stitching the edges. So rather than the appliqué sitting proud, it is slightly lower than the surface of the main fabric. A combination of standard and reverse appliqué gives a project even more depth.

1 Iron fusible interfacing to the back of the main fabric where the appliqué will be. Then pin the appliqué fabric, right side down onto the back of the interfaced fabric.

2 Draw the appliqué motif onto the reverse of the appliqué fabric using a chalk pencil or vanishing marking pen. Straight stitch around the marked line, stitching through all the layers.

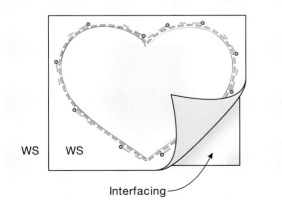

FIGURE 11 STITCH AROUND THE MOTIF THROUGH ALL THE LAYERS OF FABRIC.

3 Turn the work to the right side and, using sharp, pointed embroidery scissors, carefully snip into the top main fabric only. Cut out the appliqué shape just within the stitched lines.

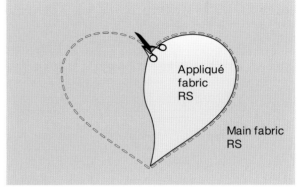

FIGURE 12 CAREFULLY CUT THE MAIN FABRIC AWAY TO REVEAL THE APPLIQUÉ BELOW.

4 Satin stitch around the shape, working from the right side so that the left swing of the stitch is in the appliqué fabric and the right swing in the main fabric.

5 If necessary, trim away any excess appliqué fabric from the reverse of the work and press.

designer
DIRECTOR'S CHAIR

EASY TO RE-COVER, DIRECTOR'S CHAIRS ARE IDEAL CANDIDATES FOR A QUICK MAKEOVER. A MATCHING SET OF REVERSIBLE COVERS WITH SOME SIMPLE APPLIQUÉ DESIGNS GIVES THIS CHAIR A STYLISH CONTEMPORARY FEEL.

PRACTISE SATIN STITCHING APPLIQUÉ MOTIFS FLAT ONTO THESE CHAIR PANELS OR EXPERIMENT WITH A THREE-DIMENSIONAL EFFECT TO LEAVE SOME OF THE SHAPES SOFTLY DETACHED FROM THE BACKGROUND. FLOWER MOTIFS LOOK PARTICULARLY FRESH ON CHAIRS FOR THE GARDEN, BUT YOU CAN CHOOSE ANY SIMPLE SHAPES FOR STRIKING RESULTS.

YOU WILL NEED
(per chair)

✓ ½yd (50cm) of main 54in- (137cm-) wide soft furnishing fabric
✓ ½yd (50cm) of complementary 54in- (137cm-) wide soft furnishing fabric
✓ Dressmaker's pattern or brown parcel paper
✓ Scraps of fabric for appliqué
✓ Double-sided fusible web
✓ Threads to match appliqué fabrics
✓ 1 reel of matching general-purpose sewing thread
✓ Sharp embroidery scissors
✓ Basic sewing kit (see p. 8)
Note: ¾yd (75cm) of fabric of each type will be sufficient for two chairs.

TECHNICAL KNOW-HOW
Creating standard satin-stitched appliqué (see p. 47)

MAKING PAPER PATTERNS

Use pattern or parcel paper to make patterns for the seat and chair back. For a standard director's chair, measure and draw up a rectangle 19¾in wide by 17in deep (48.5 x 43.5cm) for the seat cover. Measure and draw up a rectangle 21¼in wide by 8in deep (55 x 20.5cm) for the back cover. These measurements allow for ¾in (2cm) for seam allowances and casings. Mark each pattern piece with 'Cut 2'.

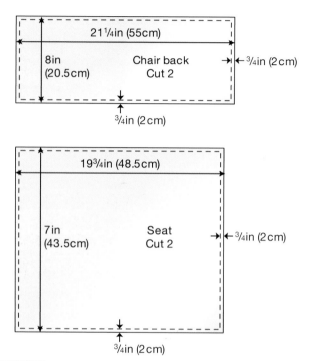

FIGURE 1 MARK THE INSTRUCTIONS ON YOUR PAPER PATTERNS CLEARLY SO THAT YOU CAN USE THEM AGAIN AND AGAIN.

EXPERT TIP

IF YOU ARE NOT SURE IF YOUR CHAIR IS THE STANDARD SIZE AND YOU HAVE OLD COVERS TO HAND, MEASURE THEM, ADDING ¾IN (2CM) TO EACH EDGE FOR SEAM ALLOWANCES.

CUTTING OUT

1 With the main fabric laid right side up on a flat surface, place the chair seat and back templates on the fabric, ready to cut one of each piece. If the fabric has a dominant design, make sure the templates are placed to show it off, for example, centring flowers or stripes. Cut out one of each shape.

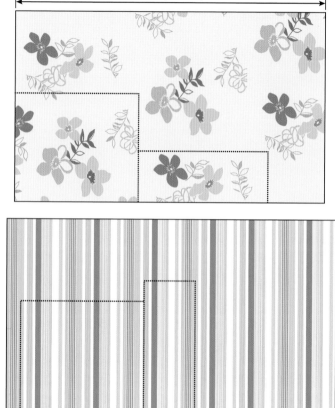

FIGURE 2 POSITION THE TEMPLATES SO THE FABRIC DESIGNS WILL LOOK MOST ATTRACTIVE ON THE CHAIR PANELS.

2 Repeat the process, using the same templates to cut out the second fabric and again placing them on the fabric so that any pattern is nicely positioned on the seat and chair back covers.

3 Draw the appliqué motifs onto your choice of fabrics. Then draw a rectangle or square around each shape and cut them out around these lines.

4 Iron double-sided fusible web to the wrong side of the appliqué pieces, following the manufacturer's instructions. When cool, cut out the appliqué motifs with sharp embroidery scissors (unless making three-dimensional appliqué; see steps 1–3 opposite).

APPLYING THE APPLIQUÉ

1 Lay the appliqué pieces on the right side of the chair back fabric, avoiding the ¾in (2cm) seam allowance down both side edges. When happy with the positioning, carefully peel the paper backing from the shapes and press them in place with a hot iron. If some of the shapes will overlap, iron on the lowest one first.

2 Set the sewing machine for satin stitch, or close zigzag, with a stitch width of 3 and stitch length of 0.5. Thread the machine with thread. Test the tension and stitching on a double layer of the same fabric.

3 Satin stitch around the shapes, using thread colour to match the appliqué fabrics (see Creating standard satin-stitched appliqué on p. 47). Press.

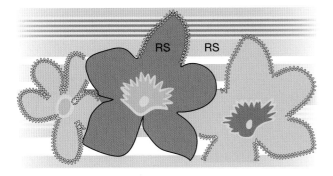

FIGURE 3 SATIN STITCH THE APPLIQUÉ IN POSITION, STARTING WITH THE UNDERLYING MOTIFS AND WORKING UP TO THE ONE ON TOP.

CREATING THREE-DIMENSIONAL APPLIQUÉ

1 Satin stitch around the edges of the motif before cutting it out of the fabric. Then trim closely around the stitching, using sharp embroidery scissors.

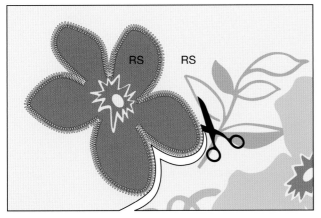

FIGURE 4 CUT THE MOTIF OUT AFTER SATIN STITCHING AROUND THE EDGES TO CREATE THREE-DIMENSIONAL APPLIQUÉ.

2 Iron a small square of double-sided fusible webbing to the centre of the appliqué piece on the wrong side. Peel the paper backing away and iron the motif in place on the chair back panel.

3 Using straight stitch in a colour to match the appliqué fabric, stitch six to eight stitches out from the flower centre and then reverse along the same stitches. With the needle down, raise the presser foot, pivot the fabric, lower the presser foot and repeat until you have stitched five or six lines in a star shape to hold the centre of the motif in place. This technique works particularly well on flower motifs as the central stitching looks like stamen. Press.

FIGURE 5 STRAIGHT STITCH THE APPLIQUÉ IN A STAR SHAPE FROM THE CENTRE.

MAKING UP THE CHAIR BACK COVER

1 With right sides together, pin the chair back pieces together matching raw edges all around. Stitch the side seams with a straight stitch and ¾in (2cm) seam allowance, reinforcing the stitching at the start and end with reverse stitching. Press the seam allowances open.

2 Refold the fabric so one seam is uppermost and then turn under the seam allowance on both long edges. Mark 2in (5cm) on each side of the seam and stitch the top seam allowance in place from mark to mark. Secure the bottom seam allowance in the same way.

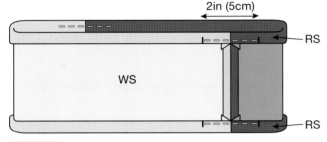

FIGURE 6   STITCH THE TOP AND BOTTOM SEAM ALLOWANCES IN PLACE ACROSS BOTH SIDE SEAMS.

3 Clip the top and bottom seam allowances vertically just beyond the stitching. Repeat from step 2 to stitch and neaten the seam allowances at the top and bottom of the other seam. Open out the unstitched allowances.

FIGURE 7   CLIP ACROSS THE SEAM ALLOWANCES.

4 With the side seams at the side edges and with right sides together, stitch across the top edge, taking a ¾in (2cm) seam allowance and starting and finishing the seam at the turned down openings. Repeat for the bottom edge, leaving a 4in (10cm) opening for turning.

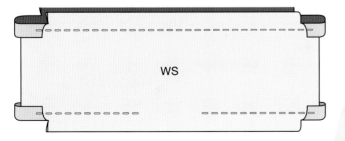

FIGURE 8   STITCH THE TOP AND BOTTOM SEAMS, LEAVING A TURNING FOR OPENING.

5 Press the seams and turn the cover through. Press it again, tucking the raw edges of the opening inside. Slip stitch the opening closed.

6 Measure and mark 1¾in (4.5cm) in from each side edge at the top and bottom of the cover. Draw two vertical chalk lines to connect each top mark to the mark directly below. Then top stitch along each line to form two casings for the chair back struts.

MAKING UP THE CHAIR SEAT COVER

Repeat steps 1-6 above, using the chair seat fabric, but top stitching ⅝in (1.5cm) from the side edges to form narrow casings for the wooden dowels which slot into the grooves on the chair.

MORE DESIGN IDEAS

- Choose different fabrics for the chair back and seat covers.
- Appliqué a name on the chair back cover.
- Make covers from a single layer of strong canvas by adding 2in (5cm) to each side edge of the chair back cover and 1in (2.5cm) to each side edge of the seat cover for the casings.

SEWING CURVED SEAMS AND ADDING BINDINGS

SEWING AND FINISHING CURVED SEAMS AND EDGES CAN MAKE ALL THE DIFFERENCE TO THE FINAL LOOK OF A PROJECT AND, OF COURSE, IT'S EASY WHEN YOU KNOW HOW. ADDING BIAS BINDING IS AN EXCELLENT WAY TO ENCASE RAW EDGES AND PROVIDE A DECORATIVE FINISH. IT IS OFTEN FOUND ON SOFT FURNISHINGS SUCH AS TIEBACKS, TABLECLOTHS AND PLACEMATS . THE CIRCULAR TABLECLOTH ON PP. 62–67, WITH ITS POCKETS AND MATCHING APPLIQUÉD NAPKINS, USES A PRETTY FLORAL FABRIC THAT WILL ADD A TOUCH OF ELEGANCE TO YOUR DINING EXPERIENCE.

TOOLS AND EQUIPMENT

✓ Ready-made bias binding or fabric to make it

✓ Bias binding maker (optional)

✓ Rotary cutter, cutting ruler and mat (optional)

✓ Basic sewing kit (see p. 8)

BIAS BINDING OPTIONS

- Bias binding can be made of any light- to medium-weight fabric. The best advice is to use a fabric that is compatible with the main fabric for the project.
- Cottons, silk and satin all make good bindings.
- Although ready-made bindings are available in different widths and fabrics, making your own means you can choose the fabric to match the project perfectly and easily make the length of binding required.
- The width of binding depends on the thickness of fabric to be bound. A ¾in (2cm) binding is suitable for a wide variety of purposes.

SEWING SENSE

Binding strips are usually cut on the bias (see p. 26). This makes them stretchy so they will curve and lie flat without rippling. It also prevents the fabric from fraying too much.

BIAS BINDING MAKER

SEWING CURVED SEAMS

Curved seams will look perfectly smooth and unpuckered if they are handled correctly. This means finishing the seam allowance in a slightly different way to straight edge seam allowances.

CLIPPING INNER CURVES

Around inner (concave) curves clip the seam allowance close to but not through the stitching. Clip regularly and at an angle to the seam. When the fabric is turned through to the right side, the seam allowance will then spread and lay flat.

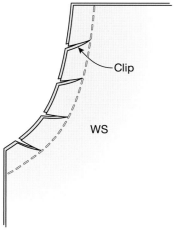

FIGURE 1 CLIP ACROSS THE SEAM ALLOWANCE AT AN ANGLE AND CLOSE TO THE STITCHING.

NOTCHING OUTER CURVES

Around outer (convex) curves notch the seam allowance by cutting out tiny wedge-shaped pieces of the fabric. This allows the seam allowance to close up and lay flat when the fabric is turned through to the right side.

FIGURE 2 CUT LITTLE NOTCHES REGULARLY AROUND AN OUTER CURVE.

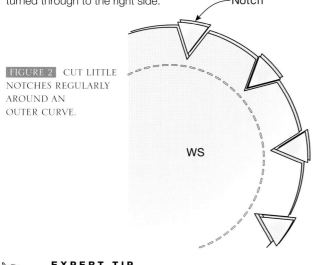

EXPERT TIP

IF USING BULKY FABRICS, IT IS A GOOD IDEA TO GRADE THE SEAM ALLOWANCES. TRIM ONE SEAM ALLOWANCE SO THAT IT IS SLIGHTLY NARROWER THAN THE ONE THAT WILL LIE CLOSEST TO THE MAIN FABRIC (SEE P. 18).

GATHERING CURVED EDGES

To help curved hems lay flat, first stitch a gathering stitch (see p. 18) just inside the hem allowance. Then very gently gather around the curved area so the right side of the fabric remains flat, but the hem allowance is slightly gathered.

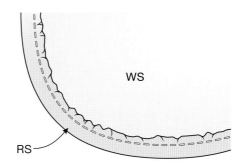

FIGURE 3 GATHER THE HEM ALLOWANCE TO EASE THE FABRIC AROUND A CURVED EDGE.

MAKING BIAS BINDING

If you need a lot of bias binding, you can either join the bias strips individually as in step 3 on p. 60 or make a continuous strip (see p. 60).

1 To find the true bias, lay the fabric flat with the selvages running down the left and right sides. Fold the cut edge of the fabric to meet one selvedge and crease along the diagonal line.

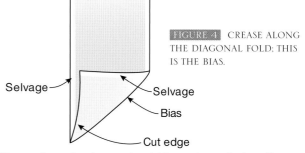

FIGURE 4 CREASE ALONG THE DIAGONAL FOLD; THIS IS THE BIAS.

2 Use a ruler and water- or air-soluble pen to mark along the fold line. Working from that line, mark parallel lines the width required for the strips. For a ¾in (2cm) finished binding, cut strips 2in (5cm) wide. Cut the strips with shears or a rotary cutter, which is quicker and more accurate.

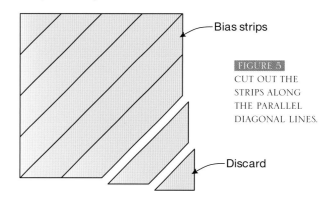

FIGURE 5 CUT OUT THE STRIPS ALONG THE PARALLEL DIAGONAL LINES.

3 Join the short ends of the strips together, with ¼in (6mm) seam allowances, to form a continuous length of binding. Pin the ends, right sides together, so the strips are at right angles. Machine sew them together at a 45-degree angle from the outside edge at the top of the overlapped strips to the outside edge at the bottom. Press the seam allowances to one side and trim. Press the seam allowances flat and open out the strip to form a continuous length. Alternatively, see the section on making continuous bias binding opposite.

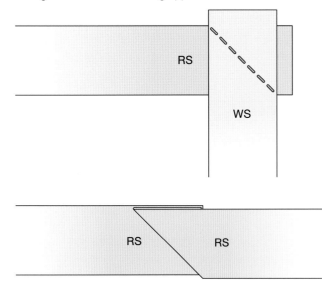

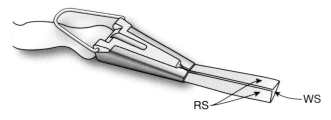

FIGURE 6 SEW THE STRIPS TOGETHER ON A 45-DEGREE ANGLE AND THEN PRESS THE SEAM FLAT.

4 Fold the strip of fabric in half lengthways, wrong sides together, and press. Fold the long edges in again to meet the original fold line or, for a wide binding, by ¼in (6mm) along each edge. Alternatively, feed the fabric strip, right side down, through the open side of a bias binding maker. Work on an ironing board and press the folded fabric as you pull it out of the binding maker to set the folds in place.

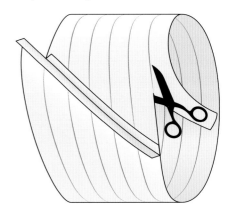

FIGURE 7 PRESS THE FOLDS AS YOU PULL THE BINDING FROM THE BINDING MAKER.

> **EXPERT TIP**
> TO START FEEDING THE FABRIC STRIP THROUGH THE BINDING MAKER, CUT THE END TO A POINT AND PUSH IT IN WITH A PIN.

MAKING CONTINUOUS BIAS BINDING

1 Fold the fabric to find the bias and mark out the strips as in steps 1 and 2 on p. 59.

2 With right sides together, fold the fabric into a tube, matching the marked lines so that one width of binding extends beyond the edge on each side. Sew the ends together with a small ¼in (6mm) seam. Press the seam open.

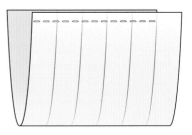

FIGURE 8 STITCH THE ENDS OF THE BINDING TOGETHER.

3 Starting at one end, cut along the marked lines, carefully working your way around the tube and cutting one long continuous strip of binding.

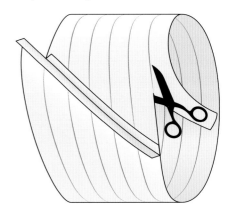

FIGURE 9 CUT ALONG THE LINES TO PRODUCE A CONTINUOUS STRIP OF BINDING.

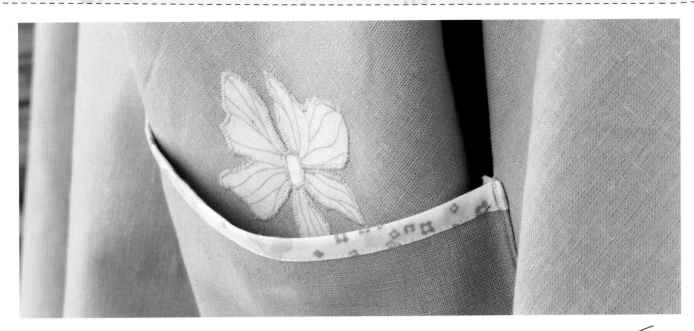

APPLYING BIAS BINDING

Bias binding can be finished by slip stitching it in place on the wrong side of the main fabric or, for speedier results, stitched 'in the ditch' from the right side.

1 Open out one long edge of the binding and pin it to the main fabric, right sides together, matching the raw edges. Stitch along the fold line nearest to the raw edges.

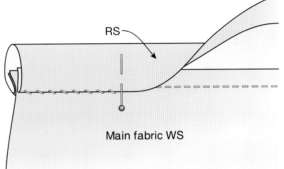

FIGURE 11 SLIP STITCH THE BINDING JUST BEYOND THE PREVIOUS STITCHING.

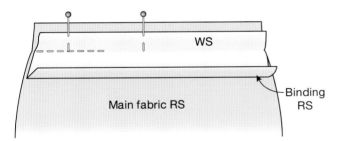

FIGURE 10 STITCH THE BINDING TO THE MAIN FABRIC ALONG THE FOLD.

2 Trim the seam allowances to a scant ⅛in (3mm), clipping and notching around any curves (see p. 59). Fold the binding over the raw edges to the wrong side of the main fabric so the second fold of the binding is just over the previous stitching. Pin the folded edge in place.

3 Slip stitch the folded edge to the wrong side of the main fabric. Alternatively, machine stitch from the right side of the main fabric, stitching in the ditch (see p. 20) while catching the binding in place. Stitch exactly where the binding joins the main fabric, gently pulling them apart as much as possible so the stitches sink into the 'ditch'.

JOINING ENDS

When a project is bound all the way around, the bias binding ends need to be joined very neatly to give a professional finish.

1 Fold the raw edge of one short end of the binding to the wrong side and press. Starting with this folded end, pin the binding to the project as in steps 1 and 2 opposite.

2 When you get back to the start position, overlap the second end of binding over the folded end by about ¾in (2cm). Finish the binding as in step 3 opposite. Once the binding is stitched and turned, only the neatened end will be visible at the join.

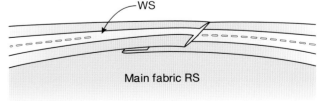

FIGURE 12 POSITION THE RAW END OF THE BINDING OVER THE FOLDED END.

delicious
DINING STYLE

THIS CIRCULAR APPLIQUÉD
TABLECLOTH IS IDEAL FOR COVERING
UP UNSIGHTLY TABLES AS THE SOFTLY
DRAPED SKIRT FALLS NEARLY TO THE
FLOOR. ADD POCKETS AND NAPKINS —
AND YOU HAVE A COMPLETE SET FOR
BREAKFAST. YOU COULD REPEAT THE
APPLIQUÉ DESIGN ON THE NAPKINS OR
USE THE SAME FABRIC AS THE BIAS
BINDING TO PROVIDE A
PRETTY CONTRAST.

FABRIC CALCULATION

1 For the table cloth, measure:
- the diameter of the table top
- the circumference of the table top
- the height, from the table top to the floor.

Multiply the height by 5½ and then add the diameter to give the total length of fabric needed. You will need to buy fabric of a width that is at least half the circumference of the table top.

SEWING SENSE
Make the paper patterns for the tablecloth to make your calculations more accurately before buying the fabric.

2 For each napkin, allow an additional 20in (50cm) square of main or contrasting fabric.

YOU WILL NEED

✓ Main fabric (see fabric calculation)
✓ 1yd (1m) contrast print fabric for appliqué and bias binding
✓ Pattern drafting paper for tablecloth pattern
✓ Pencil and string
✓ Adhesive tape (optional)
✓ 1 reel of matching general-purpose sewing thread
✓ Fusible web for appliqué
✓ Cardboard for pocket template
✓ Machine embroidery thread for appliqué
✓ Rotary cutter, cutting ruler and mat (optional)
✓ Bias binding maker (optional)
✓ Basic sewing kit (see p. 8)

TECHNICAL KNOW-HOW
Embellishing with appliqué (pp. 46–51)
Making and applying bias binding (pp. 59–61)
Edge stitching (p. 20)
Top stitching (p. 20)

MAKING THE PAPER PATTERNS

In order for the tablecloth to fit accurately, take measurements from the table and use them to make a paper pattern.

PATTERN FOR THE TABLE TOP

1 Draw the diameter of the tabletop across the pattern paper, leaving at least half the diameter measurement above and below the line. Mark the centre point on the line. From the centre, measure and mark half the diameter (radius) length at regular intervals. Join up the marks to create a circle. Add a seam allowance of ⅝in (1.5cm) around the outer edge.

Alternatively, use a large sheet of pattern paper at least the diameter of the table top plus 2in (5cm). Fold the paper in half and half again to find the centre point. Fix a length of string to the centre point with a drawing pin. Attach a pencil to the other end of the string, so the length is exactly the same as half the diameter of the table. Keeping the string taut, mark out a circle with the pencil. Add a 5/8in (1.5mm) seam allowance all around the outer edge.

PATTERN FOR THE SKIRT

1 To make the pattern for the skirt, draw a rectangle on pattern paper: the width is a quarter of the circumference of the table top and the length is the height of the tabletop from the floor minus 3/8in (1cm).

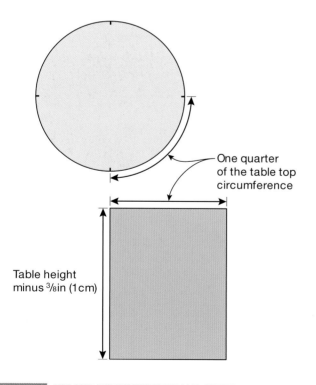

One quarter
of the table top
circumference

Table height
minus ⅜in (1cm)

FIGURE 1 USE THE CIRCUMFERENCE AND HEIGHT MEASUREMENTS TO START TO CREATE THE SKIRT PATTERN.

2 Divide the rectangle into ten equal strips across the width. Cut along the marked lines almost to the top edge to produce ten narrow strips. Working on a large sheet of paper and a flat surface, and keeping the top edges together, move the strips apart along the lower edge to make a large fan-like shape. Make sure the space between each strip is the same measurement as the width of one strip. When the strips are in place, stick them to the lower sheet of paper with adhesive tape or draw around the new outline.

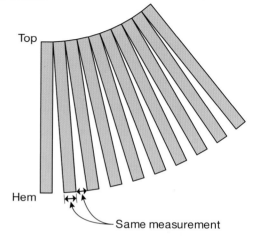

Top

Hem

Same measurement

FIGURE 2   FAN OUT THE LOWER EDGE OF THE STRIPS.

SEWING SENSE

If you don't have sheets of pattern paper large enough, stick sheets of parcel paper or wallpaper together to make a large sheet.

3 Finally, add 5/8in (1.5cm) seam allowances to the upper edge and sides but not to the hem edge. Draw a grainline parallel to one side edge and add the number of pieces to cut.

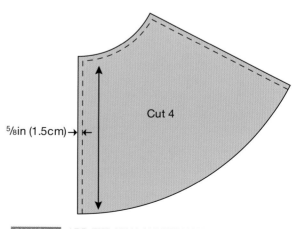

⅝in (1.5cm) →

Cut 4

FIGURE 3   ADD THE SEAM ALLOWANCES AND INSTRUCTIONS TO THE PATTERN.

EXPERT TIP

PLACING ONE SIDE SEAM ALONG THE STRAIGHT GRAIN WILL ENSURE THE SKIRT DRAPES WELL.

PATTERN FOR THE POCKET

Trace the pocket template on p. 142, transferring the seam allowance and instructions. Also cut a template from card, with all the seam allowances removed.

MAKING THE TABLECLOTH

1 Cut out one top and four skirt pieces from the main fabric, using your paper patterns. Remember to cut out the skirt pieces with the straight grain along one side seam.

SEWING SENSE

Fold the fabric in half, right sides together, and cut two skirt pieces at a time.

2 Decorate the table top piece with appliqué (see pp. 46–51). You could apply a ring of flowers using contrasting fabric or your own design. A template for the flower shape used here can be found on p. 142.

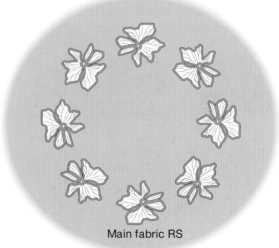

Main fabric RS

FIGURE 4 STITCH AROUND THE APPLIQUÉ SHAPES WITH MACHINE SATIN STITCH.

3 Cut out two pockets using your pattern. Place one pocket piece face down on the ironing board with the card template on top, centred but matching the upper edges. Press the raw side and bottom edges over the template to form the curved shape of the pocket, clipping into the seam allowance around the curves to help the fabric lay flat. Trim the top edge with bias binding made from contrast fabric (see Bias binding techniques, pp. 59–61). Repeat, to complete the second pocket.

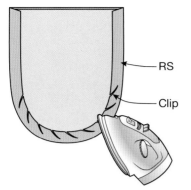

FIGURE 5 CLIP AND PRESS THE EDGES AROUND THE CURVED
SHAPE OF THE POCKET.

4 Place one pocket on a skirt panel about 5in (13cm) down from the top edge and pin it in place. Edge stitch around the sides and bottom, stitching 1/8in (3mm) from the edge and finishing with bar tacks, stitching back and forth across the top three or four times, for added strength. Repeat, stitching the other pocket onto another skirt panel.

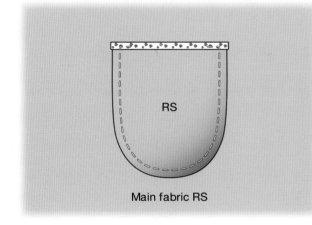
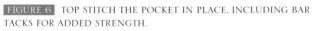

FIGURE 6 TOP STITCH THE POCKET IN PLACE, INCLUDING BAR
TACKS FOR ADDED STRENGTH.

5 Sew the skirt panels together with right sides facing, positioning the panels with pockets in the sequence desired. Match the seams cut on the straight grain first, then sew the remaining seams to create a full circle. Press the finished seams open and neaten with zigzag stitch.

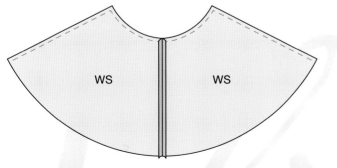

FIGURE 8 SEW THE STRAIGHT GRAIN SEAMS TOGETHER FIRST.

6 Fold the table top piece in half and half again to make equal quarters. Mark the quarter points on the outer edge with pins or marker pen. With right sides together, match up the quarter marks on the top with the seams on the skirt. Pin and sew the panels together, and then neaten with zigzag stitch. Finish the lower hem edge with bias binding cut from contrast fabric.

MAKING THE NAPKINS

Make matching napkins from the same fabric as the tablecloth, decorating each one with one or two appliquéd flowers. Finish the outer edges with bias binding or make a rolled hem stitch with the serger.

MORE DESIGN IDEAS

• Make the top of the tablecloth in a contrasting fabric with appliqué in the skirt fabric.
• Add piping between the table top and the skirt (see piping techniques, p. 79).
• Make a tablecloth for a special occasion; for example, appliqué a huge bow on the tablecloth.
• Add a shorter overskirt in contrast fabric, joining the skirts together before stitching them to the top panel.
• Make napkins from the same fabric as the bias binding on the tablecloth.

MAKING RUFFLES AND TUCKS

RUFFLES AND TUCKS ADD SURFACE INTEREST TO SOFT FURNISHINGS. THE GATHERED FOLDS OF FABRIC IN RUFFLES GIVE A SOFT EFFECT, WHICH IS OFTEN USED AS A DECORATIVE HEM EDGE. TUCKS ARE DEFINED WITH CRISP RAISED EDGES, WHICH GIVE A MUCH MORE TAILORED LOOK.

THE FABRIC-COVERED FOAM CUBE ON PP. 72–75 USES BOTH TECHNIQUES TO GOOD EFFECT TO CREATE SEATING THAT IS EASY TO MAKE AND FUN TO USE.

TOOLS AND EQUIPMENT

✓ Fine cord
✓ Marking pencil
✓ Ruler
✓ Cardboard for tuck template (optional)
✓ Basic sewing kit (see p. 8)

RUFFLE AND TUCK CHOICES

- Gather a ruffle to make a pretty skirt on a bed valance or pouffe.
- Use tucks to add style to cushion covers, pillow slips and bedspreads.
- Try sewing across a series of tucks to make them lie in different directions and add intriguing texture.

MAKING REGULAR RUFFLES

It is very easy to gather fabric and make beautiful ruffles. You can either simply sew the gathers into the seam on the bottom edge of the project or lap the top of the gathered ruffle over the hemmed edge of the project – it's a matter of personal preference. As well as gathering the fabric up along ordinary sewing thread, you can also use fine cord for this, which is ideal when working with long ruffles such as those on sofa borders.

REGULAR RUFFLES

1 Cut, or piece together, a panel of fabric 1.5–3 times the length of the straight edge it is being attached to by a suitable depth for the project. If you are attaching the ruffle to a hem, you will need a depth of fabric of about 8in (20cm). Add 1¼in (3cm) to the depth for a seam allowance and a narrow hem.

EXPERT TIP
FOR HEAVYWEIGHT FABRICS, ALLOW 1.5–2 TIMES FOR FULLNESS; FOR LIGHTWEIGHT FABRICS ALLOW 3 TIMES.

2 Hem one long edge of the ruffle panel with a narrow double hem, turning the raw edge under ⅝in (1.5cm) once and once again. Press the hem and top stitch it in place. (Alternatively, machine roll the hem using a rolled hem foot).

3 To gather the top edge of the ruffle, either hand stitch along it with long running stitches or use the longest machine straight stitch. Stitch within the seam allowance, leaving long thread tails at both ends. If you are gathering a long panel of fabric, stitch along the top edge in two or three sections, leaving just a ½in (1.3cm) gap and long thread ends between each section.

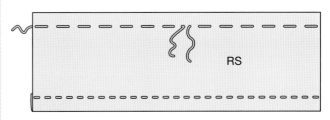

FIGURE 1 DIVIDE A LONG PANEL INTO SECTIONS SO THERE IS LESS CHANCE OF THE THREADS BREAKING WHEN YOU GATHER THE FABRIC UP.

EXPERT TIP
WHEN WORKING WITH HEAVYWEIGHT FABRICS, USE EXTRA STRONG BUTTONHOLE THREAD IN THE BOBBIN AND STITCH TWO PARALLEL ROWS OF STITCHES. PULL THE TWO BOBBIN THREADS UP TOGETHER.

4 Secure the threads at one end by wrapping them around a pin in the fabric. At the other end, gently pull up the bobbin thread to gather the fabric, moving the gathers along as you go. Continue to gather the fabric until the gathered edge is the same length as the straight edge it is to be attached to. Tie off the thread ends to keep the gathers in place.

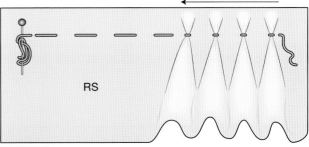

FIGURE 2 SECURE ONE END OF THE THREADS AND GATHER FROM THE OTHER END OF THE FABRIC.

EXPERT TIP
WHEN GATHERING, USE A CONTRASTING COLOUR OF THREAD IN THE BOBBIN SO IT IS EASILY IDENTIFIED.

5 With right sides together, stitch the gathered edge to the straight edge, taking a ⅝in (1.5cm) seam allowance. Neaten the raw edges. Turn the ruffle down to the right side. Press the seam allowances up and, if desired, top stitch close to the seam line to keep the seam allowances in place.

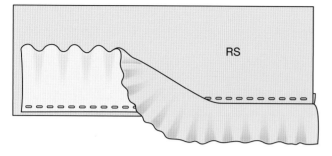

FIGURE 3 TOP STITCH CLOSE TO THE SEAM LINE IF YOU WISH.

LAPPED-TOP RUFFLES

1 Cut out the ruffle panel. Then hem both the bottom and the top edges with a double narrow hem, turning the raw edges under ⅝in (1.5cm) once and once again. Press the hems.

2 Gather the top edge as in steps 3 and 4 on p. 69.

3 Working with right sides uppermost, pin the ruffle on top of the main fabric ⅝in (1.5cm) from the hem edge, so the neatened edges match on the reverse. Top stitch the ruffle in place, stitching ¼in (6mm) from the lapped edge.

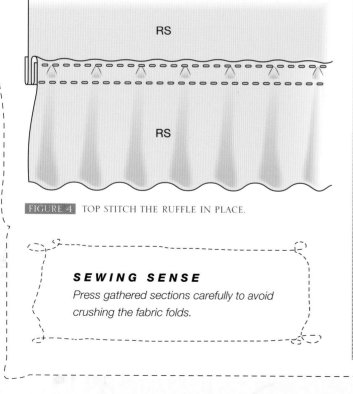

FIGURE 4 TOP STITCH THE RUFFLE IN PLACE.

SEWING SENSE
Press gathered sections carefully to avoid crushing the fabric folds.

CORD METHOD

1 Cut a length of fine cord 5in (12cm) longer than length of fabric to be gathered. Select the largest zigzag stitch width and length on your sewing machine.

2 Pin one end of the cord ¼in (6mm) from raw edge of the seam allowance on the edge to be gathered, leaving a 2in (5 cm) tail. Continue to pin the cord along its length at regular intervals. Zigzag stitch over the cord, being carefully not to catch the cord in the stitching.

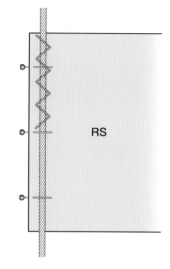

FIGURE 5 ZIGZAG OVER THE CORD, TAKING CARE THAT YOU DO NOT CATCH IT IN THE STITCHING.

3 To gather the fabric, gently pull on the cord, adjusting the gathers in the fabric. Pin and stitch the gathered panel to the main project. Remove the cord and keep it for use again.

MAKING TUCKS AND PIN TUCKS

Tucks are used in soft furnishings to provide surface interest and a textural finish. They can be adapted, making them very narrow to give pin tucks or encasing cord within the tuck to give a more prominent texture.

REGULAR TUCKS

Tucks are made by stitching folds in vertical or horizontal lines along the straight grain of the fabric. Horizontal tucks are pressed downwards, while vertical tucks can be pressed towards the centre or all in one direction.

1 Decide on the width of the tucks and then calculate the amount of fabric needed. For each tuck, allow three times the tuck width.

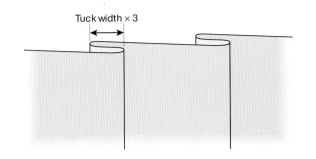

Tuck width × 3

FIGURE 6 ADD THREE TIMES THE TUCK WIDTH FOR EVERY TUCK.

2 Mark the tuck placements on the fabric. You could use a cardboard template, with notches to show the tucks and spaces between them. Clip into the seam allowance at each end of each tuck to mark the fold line; mark each stitching line with a pin.

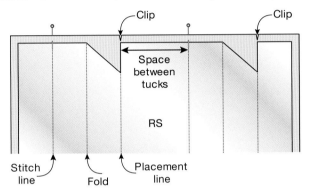

Clip

Clip

Space between tucks

RS

Stitch line

Fold

Placement line

FIGURE 7 THE CARDBOARD TEMPLATE NEEDS TO GIVE THE PLACEMENTS FOR AT LEAST TWO TUCKS AND THE SPACES ON EACH SIDE OF THEM SO YOU CAN MOVE IT ACROSS THE FABRIC TO MARK ALL THE TUCKS YOU NEED.

3 Fold the fabric along each fold line and each fold along the neighbouring stitching line. Press and stitch the tucks in place.

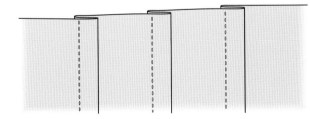

FIGURE 8 PRESS THE STITCHED TUCKS IN ONE DIRECTION.

PIN TUCKS

These narrow tucks work well on lightweight fabric with a minimal amount of folded fabric.

Mark the positions of the tucks with small snips along the top and bottom edges of the fabric. Fold and press along each tuck line. Stitch close to the fold.

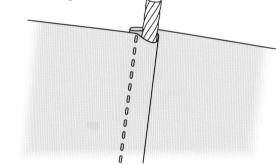

FIGURE 9 STITCH PIN TUCKS VERY CLOSE TO THE FOLDS.

CORDED TUCKS

Corded tucks form rounded ridges on the right side of the fabric. The size of the ridge depends on the width of the cord and the tuck width. For example, wider tucks will take thicker cord and therefore be more defined. Even pin tucks can be corded with fine cord to produce narrow ridges.

Mark and fold the tucks as for regular tucks. Encase cord within each fold on the wrong side of the fabric and stitch the tuck in place from the right side.

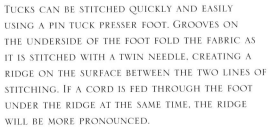

FIGURE 10 STITCH AS CLOSE TO THE CORD AS POSSIBLE.

SEWING SENSE
Stitch corded tucks with a zipper foot so you can stitch close to the cord.

EXPERT TIP
TUCKS CAN BE STITCHED QUICKLY AND EASILY USING A PIN TUCK PRESSER FOOT. GROOVES ON THE UNDERSIDE OF THE FOOT FOLD THE FABRIC AS IT IS STITCHED WITH A TWIN NEEDLE, CREATING A RIDGE ON THE SURFACE BETWEEN THE TWO LINES OF STITCHING. IF A CORD IS FED THROUGH THE FOOT UNDER THE RIDGE AT THE SAME TIME, THE RIDGE WILL BE MORE PRONOUNCED.

seriously
STYLISH SEATING

CREATE SOME CONTEMPORARY SEATING FOR A CONSERVATORY OR BEDROOM BY COVERING A FOAM CUBE. YOU COULD ADD INTEREST BY MAKING THE COVER IN FANTASTIC FABRIC OR DECORATING IT WITH APPLIQUÉ. HERE, HOWEVER, NARROW TUCKS AND GATHERED PANELS GIVE THIS COOL CUBE SOPHISTICATED TEXTURAL DETAIL.

CUTTING OUT

There are six sides to cover in fabric. Two sides and the top are cut bigger than the cube size to allow for the tucks and gathers.

- For the top, cut one panel 27½in (70cm) wide by 20in (50cm) deep
- For the bottom and two sides, cut three squares 20 x 20in (50 x 50cm)
- For the remaining two sides, cut two panels 28¾in (73cm) wide by 20in (50cm) deep.

YOU WILL NEED

✓ 2¼yd (2m) soft furnishing fabric
✓ 1–2 reels of matching general-purpose sewing thread
✓ ¾yd (50cm) twill tape
✓ 18in (46cm) foam cube
✓ 4½yd (4m) lightweight wadding or sew-in interfacing
✓ Buttonhole twist to match fabric
✓ Basic sewing kit (see p. 8)

TECHNICAL KNOW-HOW

Making pin tucks (see p. 71)
Gathering (see p. 18 and p. 69)

PREPARING THE PANELS

1 On the top panel, measure 3in (8cm) from the left edge and mark a vertical line from top to bottom. Mark and stitch seven parallel narrow tucks, pressing them all to one side (see p. 71). Measure the panel again and either make a few more tucks or cut the width down to 20in (50cm).

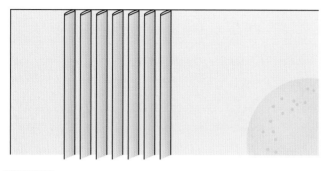

FIGURE 1 MAKE SEVEN TUCKS ON THE LEFT SIDE OF THE TOP PANEL.

2 Stitch two rows of gathering stitches along the top and bottom edges of both rectangular side panels (see steps 3 and 4 of Making regular ruffles on p. 69).

MAKING UP THE CUBE

1 With right sides together, join one of the rectangular side panels to one of the square side panels along one side edge, starting and ending the stitching ¾in (2cm) from each end of the seam. Repeat with the other pair of side panels.

2 Join both pairs of panels to form one continuous piece.

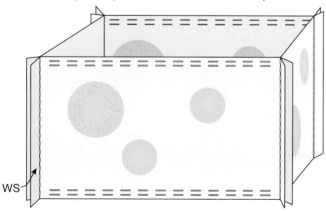

FIGURE 2 MAKE SURE THE RECTANGULAR AND THE SQUARE PANELS ARE OPPOSITE EACH OTHER.

3 With right sides together, pin the side panels around the edges of the top panel, matching the seams at the corners, carefully pulling up the gathers and distributing the fullness evenly. Stitch the panels together.

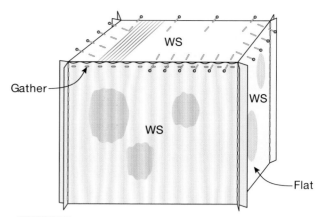

FIGURE 3 STITCH THE SIDE PANELS TO THE TOP PANEL.

4 Pin the bottom panel to the bottom edge of one of the side panels to be gathered, pulling up the gathering threads to match the side seams. Stitch just those two panels together.

5 On the remaining edge to be gathered, pull up the gathering thread until the edge is 20in (50cm). Pin and then stitch the twill tape to the wrong side of that edge.

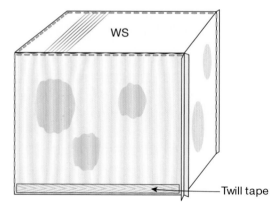

FIGURE 4 STITCH THE TWILL TAPE TO THE WRONG SIDE OF THE GATHERED PANEL.

6 Turn the cover right sides out and press it carefully. Tuck the seam allowances on the three open sides to the inside and press.

7 Wrap the foam cube in the wadding or interfacing, hand stitching any openings in the wrapping closed along the edges of the cube. Trim any excess wrapping.

8 Insert the cube into the cover. Pin the bottom panel in place on the three open sides and slip stitch it by hand using buttonhole twist thread.

MORE DESIGN IDEAS

- Use bright nursery colours to make the seat cover, keep the sides panels flat and appliqué large numbers or letters on each side before making up.
- Insert piping around the top and bottom seams.

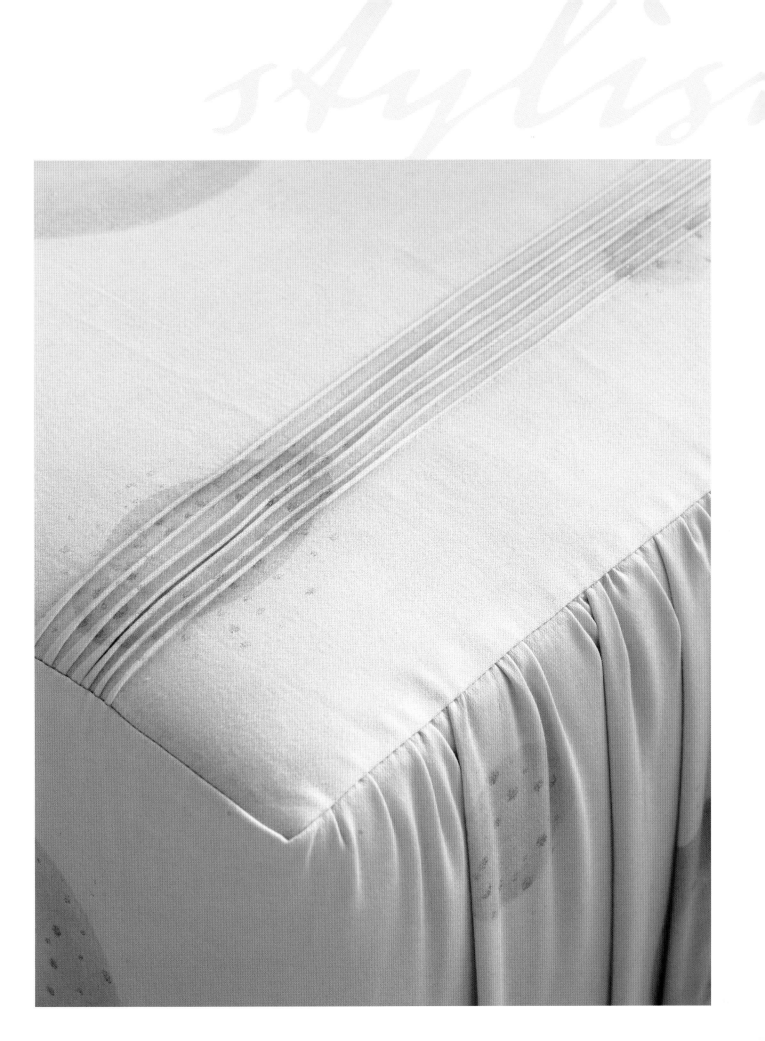

MAKING AND INSERTING PIPING

PIPING IS A RAISED TRIM THAT PROVIDES DEFINITION, DETAIL AND CRISP EDGING. IT CAN CONSIST OF READY-MADE DECORATIVE CORD ATTACHED TO TAPE, OR FLANGE, OR YOU CAN COVER PLAIN PIPING (WELTING) CORD WITH FABRIC TO MATCH OR CONTRAST WITH THE REST OF THE SLIPCOVER. BOTH ARE ATTACHED BY SEWING THEM IN BETWEEN LAYERS OF FABRIC.

PIPING (WELTING) CORD IS USUALLY WHITE AND COMES IN DIFFERENT THICKNESSES SUITABLE FOR SOFT FURNISHINGS AND DRESSMAKING. THICKER CORDS ARE USED FOR FURNISHINGS, WHILE THE FINER ONES WORK BEST FOR FASHION. IN THE PROJECT ON PP. 80—83, YOU CAN SEE HOW TO ADD PIPING TO A PADDED SEAT COVER.

FABRIC CHOICES

- Fabrics that are suitable for making piping include light- to medium-weight woven fabrics such as furnishing cottons.
- Avoid fabric that is too tightly woven or bulky as it needs to be folded in two to wrap the cord and then stitched between two layers of fabric for the slipcover.

TOOLS AND EQUIPMENT

✓ Piping cord and bias strips of fabric, OR

✓ Flanged cord

✓ Zipper foot

✓ Small scissors

✓ Basic sewing kit (see p. 8)

ATTACHING FLANGED CORD

Ready-made flanged cord is available in different thicknesses, as well as a wide variety of plain and multi-colours. It is attached to slipcovers using the in-seam method.

DIFFERENT DESIGNS OF FRINGED CORD

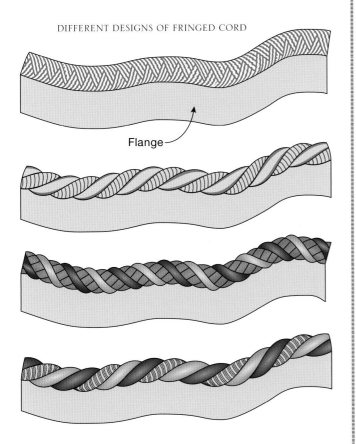

Flange

1 Pin the flanged cord to the right side of the fabric for the front of the slipcover, matching the raw edge of the fabric to the straight edge of the flange.

2 Using a zipper foot, stitch the flange to the main fabric close to the cord and within the seam allowance.

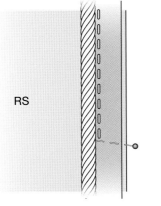

RS

FIGURE 1 SECURE THE TRIM BY STITCHING THROUGH THE FLANGE CLOSE TO THE CORD.

3 At corners and around curves, clip into the flange and bunch up the cord slightly so that it will lay flat when turned through to the right side.

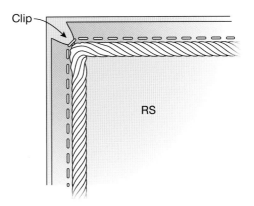

Clip

RS

FIGURE 2 CLIP INTO THE FLANGE TO EASE IT AROUND CORNERS AND CURVES.

4 Place the fabric for the back of the slipcover, right sides together over the front piece, sandwiching the cord. Pin it in place with the pins at right angles to the raw edge.

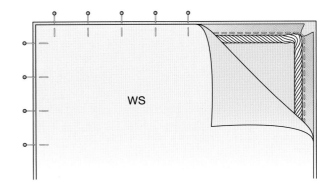

WS

FIGURE 3 PIN THE BACK PANEL IN PLACE OVER THE CORD.

5 Using the zipper foot and working with the front of the slipcover uppermost, secure all the layers by stitching to the left of the first row of stitching, closer to the cord. If possible, move the needle further to the left: turn the balance wheel of the sewing machine by hand to test the stitch position and ensure that the needle doesn't hit the presser foot.

6 Trim the seam allowances, clipping and notching around curves (see p. 59 for further guidance) before turning the slipcover through. The cord will now be on the outer edge, standing proud.

OVERLAPPING CORD ENDS

1 If the cord ends will meet, as on a cushion cover, start to attach it in an inconspicuous area or at the centre of a long edge. Position the first pin so that a short end of the cord is unattached to the fabric, curving the end so it is outside the seam allowance.

2 Pin the rest of the cord in position until you reach the beginning again. Lap the end of the cord over the original end, again curving it off the fabric edge.

3 Stitch the cord in place as described above, taking the stitching straight across the cord ends to maintain a straight line. If the trim is very bulky at the overlap, stitch this section by hand. Trim the cord ends.

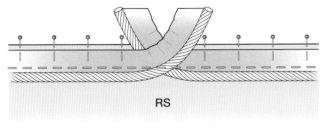

RS

FIGURE 4 OVERLAP THE ENDS OF THE CORD.

MAKING FABRIC-COVERED PIPING

If you want piping to match the main fabric perfectly or pick up accent colours in it, the best option is to cover plain piping cord with fabric. You will need to cut the fabric on the bias so it will bend and flex around curves and corners smoothly.

HOMEMADE PIPING

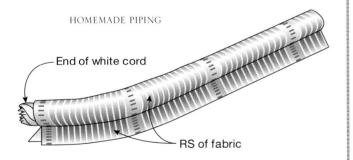

End of white cord

RS of fabric

1 Cut enough bias strips (see pp. 59–60 for cutting bias strips) to cover the length of piping cord needed to go around your project. Join the strips or make continuous bias strips as necessary. Fold the strips in half lengthways, wrong sides together, and press.

2 Lay the piping cord inside the strip against the fold. Pin or baste the long edges of fabric together.

3 Sew the piping to the main fabric, following steps 1–6 on p. 77.

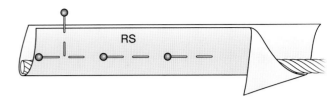

RS

FIGURE 5 PIN OR BASTE THE PIPING CORD INSIDE THE FABRIC.

OVERLAPPING PIPING ENDS

1 If the piping ends will meet, start to attach it in an inconspicuous area or at the centre of a long edge. Pin the piping in position. Where the ends meet, open the piping fabric to reveal the cord.

2 On the lower piece of piping, fold in the raw end of fabric. Trim the piping cord back so that it is shorter than the fabric by 1in (2.5cm).

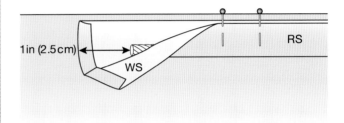

1in (2.5cm) WS RS

FIGURE 6 TRIM BACK THE CORD INSIDE THE LOWER PIECE OF PIPING FABRIC.

3 Lay the upper layer of fabric and cord on top and trim so the fabric overlaps by 1in (2.5cm) and the cord ends meet exactly.

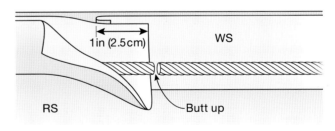

1in (2.5cm) WS RS Butt up

FIGURE 7 TRIM THE UPPER LAYER OF FABRIC AND CORD.

4 Hand stitch the cord ends together so they don't separate later. Fold the piping fabric back over the cord again and pin it in place. Stitch the piping in place (see steps 1–6 on p. 77).

box clever

BENCH SEATING

TURN A GARDEN BENCH OR WINDOW
SEAT INTO A COSY NOOK WITH SOME
COMFORTABLE PADDED SEATING. A BOX
COVER IS SIMPLE TO MAKE TO SIZE,
WHILE PIPED EDGES GIVE A CRISP,
PROFESSIONAL FINISH. IF YOU INSERT A
ZIPPER INTO ONE LONG SIDE GUSSET,
THE COVER WILL BE EASY TO REMOVE
AND LAUNDER.

CONSIDER USING WATER-RESISTANT
FABRIC IF YOU ARE MAKING SEATING
FOR AN OUTDOOR CHAIR AND SEAL
THE SEAMS WITH A SEAM-SEALANT GEL.

MATERIALS CALCULATION

1 If the seat is rectangular, measure the width and length. If it is shaped, use parcel paper and draw around the seat. Fold the paper in half and cut out the shape so it is symmetrical. Then place the paper pattern on the chair seat to check the fit.

2 Decide how deep the cushion will be, for example, 4in (10cm) is a comfortable depth.

3 For the fabric, you will need:

- 2 x the dimensions of the seat, plus ¾in (2cm) seam allowances all around
- gusset strip (see step 3 on p. 82), plus seam allowances as above
- zipper gusset (see step 4 on p. 84), plus seam allowances as above
- ½yd (50cm) to make the piping
- any extra fabric for pattern matching or placement on the cover.

4 Have a piece of seating-quality foam cut to the size and shape required, using the pattern or measurements as necessary.

YOU WILL NEED

✓ Upholstery furnishing fabric (see calculations above)
✓ Seating-quality foam pad (see calculations above)
✓ Parcel paper or wallpaper lining (to make pattern)
✓ 4oz (115g) polyester wadding to wrap foam pad
✓ Stockinette to slip over foam pad
✓ 1–2 reels of matching general-purpose sewing thread
✓ Zipper approximately the length of the seat
✓ Spray adhesive (optional)
✓ Basic sewing kit (see p. 8)

TECHNIQUES USED

- Making and inserting piping (pp.76–79)
- Inserting zippers (pp. 84–87)
- Making ties (pp. 40–41)

PREPARING THE CUSHION PAD

1 Cut a length of wadding to wrap around the foam pad, so the ends butt together along one edge. Either use spray adhesive to secure the wadding around the foam or hand sew the ends together using large stitches.

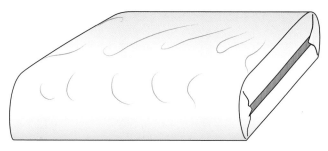

FIGURE 1   WRAP THE FOAM PAD WITH A LAYER OF WADDING.

2 Cut a piece of stockinette to the required length and insert the wrapped foam pad. Stitch the open ends of the stockinette by hand to secure.

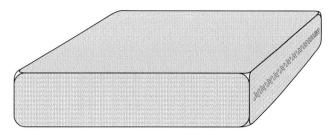

FIGURE 2   SLIP THE FOAM PAD INTO A LENGTH OF STOCKINETTE.

EXPERT TIP
THE WADDING FORMS THE CROWN OF THE SEAT AND ENSURES THE COVER WILL FIT SNUGLY.

MAKING THE CUSHION COVER

1 Using the seat measurements or the paper pattern, add ¾in (2cm) all around for seam allowances. Cut two pieces of fabric, for the top and bottom of the cover, placing any fabric pattern in the centre of each piece. Mark the centre front and centre back edges with notches.

EXPERT TIP
IF YOU NEED TO JOIN FABRIC TO MAKE THE TOP AND BOTTOM PANELS OF THE COVER, CONSIDER POSITIONING THE WIDEST PIECE OF FABRIC AS THE CENTRE PANEL WITH TWO NARROWER STRIPS ON THE OUTER EDGES.

2 Make up enough piping to go all around the top and bottom edges of the wrapped foam pad. Attach the piping to the right side edges of the top and bottom pieces of fabric (see Making and inserting piping, pp. 76–79). Set these pieces aside.

3 For the length of the gusset strips, measure the two side and the front edges of the cushion pad and deduct 2½in (6.5cm) from the total length. For the width of the strips, measure the depth of the pad and add 1½in (4cm) for seam allowances. If possible cut one strip of fabric to these measurements. If the cushion is very long, you may need to join a strip to each end to get the required length. Mark the centre of each long edge.

EXPERT TIP
IF THE FABRIC HAS A DISTINCTIVE PATTERN, YOU MAY WANT TO MATCH THE PATTERN ON THE GUSSET TO THE PATTERN ON THE TOP PANEL.

EXPERT TIP

IF THE BENCH SEAT IS QUITE LONG, A CONTINUOUS ZIPPER IS ADVISABLE. FIRST CUT IT TO THE CORRECT LENGTH. THEN BAR TACK (SEE P. 15) ACROSS BOTH ENDS, USING DOUBLE THREAD OR BUTTONHOLE TWIST, TO PREVENT THE ZIPPER PULL FROM COMING OFF.

4 For the zipper gusset, measure the back edge of the cushion pad and add 5½in (14cm). Cut two strips across the fabric to this length by the width decided in step 3 on p. 82. Mark the centre of each long edge. Fold each zipper gusset piece lengthways and right sides together, and press. Cut a piece of continuous zipper to this length. Insert the zipper, stitching the zipper tape along each of the folded edges (see Inserting zippers, pp. 84–87).

5 Join the zipper gusset to the rest of the gusset strip, taking ¾in (2cm) seam allowances, to make a circular piece.

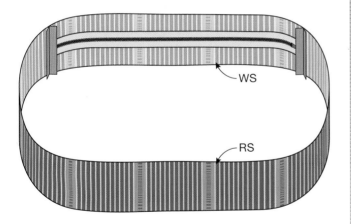

FIGURE 3 JOIN THE ZIPPER GUSSET TO THE REST OF THE GUSSET TO MAKE ONE CONTINUOUS PIECE.

6 With right sides together, pin the gusset to the cover top, matching the centre notches. Sew them together, stitching as close to the piping as possible by using a zipper foot and clipping the gusset at the corners and around curves as necessary.

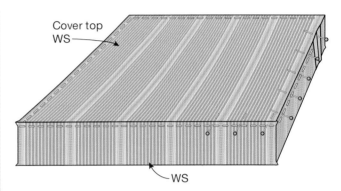

FIGURE 4 PIN AND SEW THE GUSSET TO THE COVER TOP.

7 Open the zipper, and then attach the cover bottom as in step 6. Turn the cover through the zipper opening and insert the pad.

ADDING CUSHION TIES

If the cushion is for a chair seat or for a bench with open slats on the back, you could add ties to the back of the cover to hold the cushion in place. Make the ties 13in (33cm) long for garden chairs and benches.

Before stitching the cover bottom and the gusset pieces together, make up and insert the ties into the seam (see pp. 40–41 on how to make and insert ties). Alternatively, allow for seams in the gusset at the appropriate place for ties and insert them in the centre of the gusset seams.

MORE DESIGN IDEAS

• Make the top and bottom of the cover in different fabrics so they can be used either way up to ring the changes.

• Add self-covered buttons to the cushion. Use buttonhole thread to stitch the buttons to the top of the cover, taking the threads through the foam to the underside and tying them off tightly before stitching the bottom cover section to the gusset.

INSERTING ZIPPERS

THERE ARE THREE MAIN WAYS TO INSERT A
REGULAR ZIPPER INTO SOFT FURNISHINGS —
THEY CAN BE CENTRED, LAPPED OR
INVISIBLE. ZIPPERS CAN BE USED AS A
FASTENING ON SEATING, CUSHION COVERS
AND CHAIR COVERS. WITH A ZIPPER,
SLIPCOVERS CAN EASILY BE REMOVED
FOR LAUNDERING.

THE EASE OF LAUNDERING COMES
INTO PLAY ESPECIALLY WHEN SOFT
FURNISHINGS ARE USED ON THE FLOOR!
THE BEANBAG ON P. 88–91 IS SUCH A FUN
PROJECT TO MAKE, AND TO PERSONALIZE
WITH YOUR OWN DESIGN, BUT THE ZIPPER
CERTAINLY HELPS TO MAKE THIS SEATING
VERY PRACTICAL TOO.

ZIPPER CHOICES

- Choose a zipper in a similar colour to the main fabric.
- Zippers come in various weights, with different strengths and teeth size. Use a metal zipper with heavyweight fabric, especially if it will be under pressure, and a lightweight nylon zip for light- to medium-weight fabrics.
- If the correct zipper length isn't available, you could shorten a longer one. See the guidelines on p. 87.

TOOLS AND EQUIPMENT

✓ Zipper of appropriate length

✓ Zipper foot

✓ Basic sewing kit (see p. 8)

CENTRING A ZIPPER

The easiest method of inserting a zipper is to centre it under the butting edges of the project, so that the fabric covers the zipper teeth. The stitching shows on the right side of the project.

1 Pin the seam, right sides together. Position the closed zipper so the teeth are centred over the pinned seam. Mark the position of the metal base of the zipper on the seam allowance.

2 Remove the zipper and baste the seam from the top to the mark, using the longest stitch length. Change to regular stitch length and stitch the rest of the seam, reverse stitching at the start and end of the regular stitching to secure the threads. Press the seam allowances open.

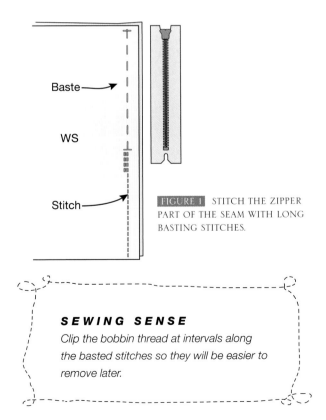

Baste

WS

Stitch

FIGURE 1 STITCH THE ZIPPER PART OF THE SEAM WITH LONG BASTING STITCHES.

3 With the work wrong side uppermost, again place the closed zipper, right side down, making sure the teeth are centred along the basted seam and the metal base is in the correct position. Pin and baste the zipper in place through all the layers. Remove the basting stitches that hold the seam closed.

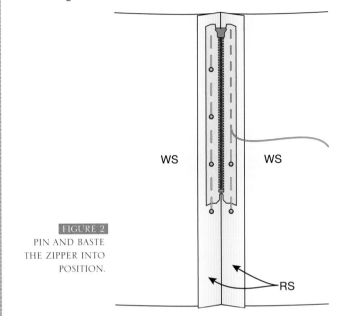

WS   WS

FIGURE 2
PIN AND BASTE
THE ZIPPER INTO
POSITION.

RS

4 Working on the right side and using the zipper foot, machine stitch from the seam at the bottom of the zipper, across the zipper tape, then pivot and stitch up the side of the zipper to the top. Stitch ¼–⅝in (6m–1.5cm) from the seam depending on the size of the zipper teeth. As you get close to the top, stop stitching and, with the needle down and the foot raised, open the zipper and work the pull past the foot. Finish stitching to the top. Repeat for the other side, again starting at the centre bottom of the zipper. Remove the basting stitches.

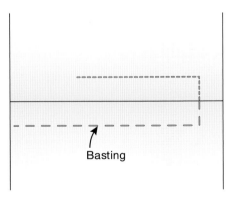

Basting

FIGURE 3 STITCH ALONG EACH SIDE OF THE ZIPPER SEAM. EACH TIME STARTING AT THE BASE OF THE ZIPPER.

INSERTING A LAPPED ZIPPER

With this method one side of the fabric overlaps the other so that only one line of stitching is visible. This is achieved by stitching one side of the zipper to the edge of the folded-under seam allowance and the other side of the zipper to the seam line so that when the zipper is closed, the fabric laps over.

1 Mark the zipper position and then baste and stitch the seam as for a centred zipper. Press the seam allowances open.

2 With the wrong side of the work uppermost, open the zipper and place it right side down so the teeth on the left side lie along the left side of the seam line and over the seam allowance. Baste the centre of the zipper tape to the seam allowance only.

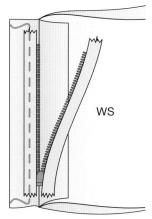

FIGURE 4 BASTE ONE SIDE OF THE ZIPPER SO THE TEETH LIE ALONG THE SEAM LINE.

3 Close the zipper and then turn it right side up, so the seam allowance folds under. Refold the seam allowance so the seam line is close to, but not touching, the zipper teeth. Using the zipper foot, machine stitch through the fold and tape as close to the teeth as possible, starting at the bottom of the zipper.

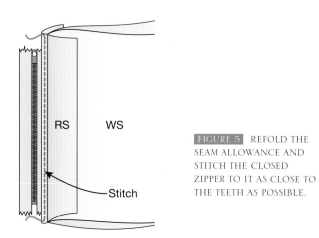

FIGURE 5 REFOLD THE SEAM ALLOWANCE AND STITCH THE CLOSED ZIPPER TO IT AS CLOSE TO THE TEETH AS POSSIBLE.

4 Clip the seam allowance below the bottom end of the zipper. Open out the work so the zipper is face down and the wrong side of the fabric uppermost. Smooth the fabric and zipper flat, checking that the zipper teeth are correctly aligned and will close easily. Baste the right-hand side of the zipper tape through all the thicknesses across the bottom and up the side about ½in (1.3cm) from the seam line.

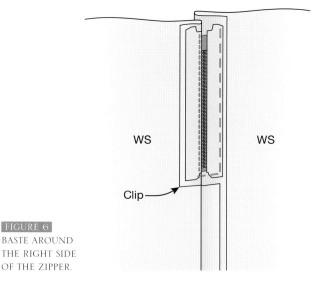

FIGURE 6 BASTE AROUND THE RIGHT SIDE OF THE ZIPPER.

5 Turn the work over and, from the right side, machine stitch along the basting, again working from the bottom to the top of the zipper and reinforcing the stitches at start and finish. Remove the basting.

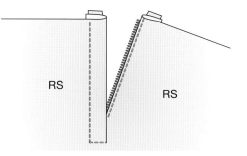

FIGURE 7 MACHINE STITCH ALONG THE BASTING STITCHES BEFORE REMOVING THEM.

INSERTING AN INVISIBLE ZIPPER

On an invisible, or concealed, zipper, the teeth are on the underside so only the zipper pull is visible on the right side. There is no stitching on show either, because you sew the zipper tape to the seam allowance. The key to inserting an invisible zipper perfectly is to use an invisible zipper foot, which probably makes it the easiest of all zipper insertions.

INVISIBLE ZIPPER FOOT

Top

Underside

An invisible zipper foot has grooves underneath it, along which the zipper teeth slide so the stitches are sewn extremely close to the teeth.

> ### SEWING SENSE
> *Buy an invisible zipper at least 1in (2.5cm) longer than required. This is because you cannot stitch right to the bottom invisibly and will effectively lose the last inch (2.5cm) of the opening.*

1 Fold the seam allowances to the wrong side along the seam line and press. Mark the position of the zipper on the seam allowance. (Unlike regular zipper insertion, do not sew the rest of the seam at this stage).

2 Open out the seam allowance. With the fabric right side up and the zipper open, place one side of the zipper tape face down on the seam allowance with the teeth along the crease. Pin the tape in place.

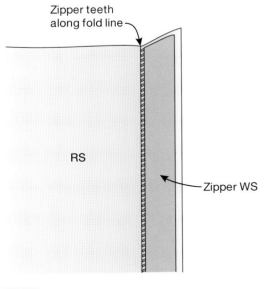

Zipper teeth along fold line

RS

Zipper WS

FIGURE 8 PIN ONE SIDE OF THE ZIPPER TAPE TO THE FABRIC.

EXPERT TIP
IF THIS METHOD IS NEW TO YOU, BASTE DOWN THE CENTRE OF THE ZIPPER TAPE AT THIS STAGE AND THEN REMOVE THE BASTING STITCHES WHEN THE ZIPPER IS SECURED.

3 Attach the invisible zipper foot. Sew from the top of the zipper with the teeth in the groove under the foot. As you stitch, gently uncurl the zipper teeth so the stitching goes under the teeth, which will curl back after being stitched. Sew as near to the bottom of the zipper as possible. Back stitch to secure.

4 Close the zipper and pin the other side of the tape in position on the other seam allowance. Make sure the placement marks match up and the teeth align with the fold along the seam line. Sew in place from top to bottom.

5 Pin the remainder of the seam, right sides together. Then using a regular zipper foot, stitch the seam starting at the base of the zipper. Back stitch at the start to strengthen the seam.

6 Fold the main fabric out of the way and anchor the zipper tape to the seam allowance, using the regular zipper foot and stitching down the centre of the tape.

SHORTENING A ZIPPER

If the correct length of zipper isn't available, buy a longer one and shorten it to the required length.

Measure the zipper from the pull at the top to the desired length and mark across the zipper. Using double thread in a matching colour, stitch eight to ten bar tacks across the zip teeth at the marked position. Cut the zipper ½in (1.3cm) below the tacks.

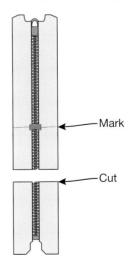

Mark

Cut

FIGURE 9 BAR TACK ACROSS THE ZIPPER TO FORM THE NEW LENGTH AND THEN TRIM THE REMAINDER AWAY.

soft and squishy
BEANBAG

TAKE A DRAMATIC FABRIC PRINT AND
AN UNUSUAL SHAPE — AND CREATE A
TOTALLY UNIQUE BEANBAG THAT WILL
BE THE ENVY OF ALL YOUR FRIENDS!
THE IDEA IS SO ADAPTABLE AND GIVES
LOTS OF SCOPE FOR USING BOLD
FABRIC OR APPLIQUÉD DECORATION
TO MAKE BAGS OF ALL SIZES FOR
SITTING ON OR FOR STORING ALL
SORTS OF BITS AND PIECES. DON'T
FORGET THAT A ZIPPER MAKES THE
PERFECT CLOSING TO ENSURE THE
COVER CAN BE LAUNDERED AND
ALWAYS LOOKS IN PRISTINE
CONDITION.

YOU WILL NEED
✓ 2½yd (2.5m) of 60in-wide (150cm-wide) heavyweight furnishing fabric
✓ 2½yd (2.5m) of 60in-wide (150cm-wide) calico or lining
✓ Pattern paper or roll of brown paper
✓ String and pencil
✓ 1 reel of matching general-purpose sewing thread
✓ 18in (46cm) zipper
✓ 14in (36cm) x ¾in-wide (2cm-wide) hook and loop fastener
✓ 1 x tassel
✓ Filling beans
✓ Basic sewing kit (see p. 8)

MEASUREMENTS
This bean bag has a 30in (76cm) diameter and is 36in (90cm) high.

TECHNICAL KNOW-HOW
Inserting zippers (see pp. 84–87)
Finishing seams (see pp. 18–19)

PREPARING THE BASE PATTERN

1 To make the pattern for the beanbag base, draw a line 30in (76cm) long on the pattern paper. Find the centre point. Wind some string around a pencil so the string measures 15in (38cm). Holding the loose end of the string on the centre and keeping the string taut, draw a semi-circle with the pencil starting at one end of the line.

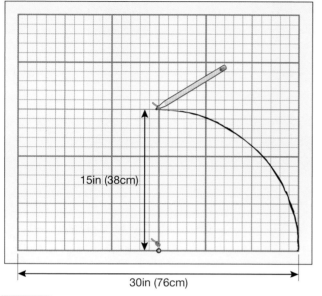

FIGURE 1 DRAW A SEMI-CIRCLE, USING THE PENCIL AND STRING.

PREPARING THE SIDE PATTERN

1 To make the pattern for the beanbag sides, take the base pattern and fold it in half, matching straight edges, to make a quarter segment. Fold it in half again to make a crease line, bringing the first fold to the straight edges. Trace around the quarter segment shape onto another piece of pattern paper also marking the crease line. Put the base pattern to one side.

2 On the new quarter segment, continue the creased centre line vertically so it measures 36in (90cm) from the lower curved edge. Add ⅝in (1.5cm) to each end of the curved edge and mark those points as A and B. Join points A and B to the top of the vertical line at C, creating a cone shape (see Figure 2). Cut out this pattern.

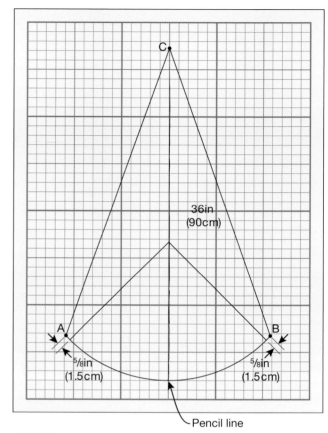

FIGURE 2 FIND AND JOIN UP POINTS A, B AND C TO MAKE A CONE-SHAPED PATTERN.

CUTTING OUT

1 Fold the fabric in half with right sides together. Using chalk, mark a 1in (2.5cm) line in from the selvages. Place the straight edge of the base pattern on the line and pin through all the layers. Cut out two base pieces. The selvages will be the seam allowance.

2 Place the side pattern on the folded fabric, lining up the vertical line along the grainline, parallel to the selvages. Cut out two side pieces. Then re-pin the pattern and cut out two more pieces, making sure the pattern or nap runs in the same direction on all four pieces.

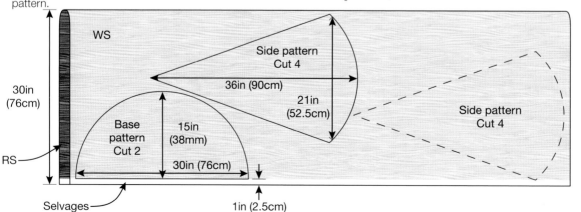

FIGURE 3 CUT OUT TWO BASE AND FOUR SIDE PIECES.

MAKING UP

1 With right sides facing, pin the base pieces together along the straight edges. Making a 1in (2.5cm) seam, baste the pieces together and press the seam open.

2 Lay the zipper centrally along the basted seam. With chalk, mark the position of the zipper pull and just above the zipper stop, making sure there is an equal amount of seam above and below the zipper. Put the zipper to one side.

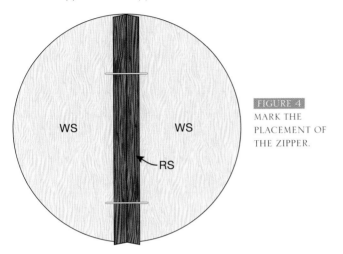

3 Machine stitch the seam above and below the zipper placement, back stitching at the marks to secure the seam and leaving the zipper placement unstitched. Press the seam again.

4 Baste the zipper in place from the wrong side and then stitch it in place from the right side, following steps 3 and 4 on p. 85.

5 With right sides together and taking ⅝in (1.5cm) seams, join the side pieces in pairs. Then join the pairs together.

6 Open the zipper and, with right sides together and taking ⅝in (1.5cm) seams, pin the lower edge of the side pieces to the outer edge of the base. Baste and then machine stitch them together. Neaten the seam allowances, clipping into them around the curves. Press and turn the beanbag to the right side through the zipper opening.

7 Sew a tassel to the top point to finish the beanbag.

MAKING THE LINING BAG

1 Using the lining fabric or calico, cut out two base and four side pieces as for the main beanbag.

2 Pin one piece of the hook and loop tape on the right side of one base piece centrally and close to the selvage. Baste and then machine it in place. Stitch the other piece of hook and loop tape

to the second base piece in the same way, making sure the tapes are in the same positions on the seam allowances so they will closethe bag when joined.

3 With fabric right sides together, press the hook and loop tape together. Pin and then stitch a 1in (2.5cm) seam above and below the tape. Press the seam allowances to one side.

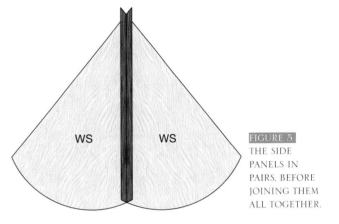

4 Continue making the lining, following steps 5 and 6 for making the main beanbag.

5 Place the lining inside the main beanbag, matching the bases and side panels. Carefully fill the lining bag with filling beans and then press the hook and loop tape closed. Zip up the outer bag.

SEWING SENSE

Always make an inner bag for the filling beans so you can easily remove the outer cushion cover for laundering. These loose beans are usually made of polystyrene and are more flexible than wadding and other types of stuffing, making them ideal for a beanbag.

MORE DESIGN IDEAS

• Make a beanbag for a child's room in primary-coloured fleece. Instead of a tassel, sew strands of black wool to the top and let it flop over like hair. Glue or stitch large felt eyes and a mouth in place to make a friendly face.

• Make a bag half the size in a nursery print. Stitch the base sections together and leave a neatened opening between two side panels. Add a ribbon loop to the top and you have a useful laundry bag or home for soft toys.

DECORATIVE STITCHING AND SURFACE EMBELLISHMENT

SOFT FURNISHINGS CAN LOOK STUNNING WHEN EMBELLISHED WITH CREATIVE STITCHING. COUCHING, DECORATIVE TOP STITCHING AND FREE-MOTION STITCHWORK CAN TOTALLY TRANSFORM A PLAIN FABRIC OR ADD FABULOUS TEXTURE TO EVEN A PATTERNED FABRIC. YOU CAN CREATE A WIDE RANGE OF EFFECTS WITH A HUGE CHOICE OF GORGEOUS CORDS, RIBBONS, THREADS, YARNS AND BEADS — THE POSSIBILITIES ARE ENDLESS.

COUCHING AND FREE-MOTION STITCHING ARE DEMONSTRATED ON THE CHARMING HEADBOARD ON PP. 96–101, WHICH IS BEAUTIFULLY FINISHED AROUND THE EDGES WITH PIPING.

MAKING EMBROIDERY CHOICES

CHOOSING NEEDLES

A machine embroidery needle has a larger than normal eye to cope with fancy embroidery threads. Specially coated needles are also available for use with metallic threads, which can wear a virtually invisible groove in a normal needle eye causing threads to shred or break. For most threads, a size 10–12 (80–90) needle is ideal, while for metallic threads, choose a size 12–14 (70–80).

CHOOSING THREADS

Most machine embroidery threads are finer than regular sewing thread and have a lovely lustre to them, so you can create concentrated areas of stitch and colour. Specialist machine threads also include metallics and variegated colors. Bobbinfill is a very fine thread, usually white or black, which is used in the bobbin and cuts down the amount of thread in densely stitched sections.

TOOLS AND EQUIPMENT

✓ Cord, ribbon or yarn

✓ Machine embroidery needles

✓ Machine embroidery threads

✓ Twin machine needles (optional)

✓ Matching or contrasting threads

✓ Gimping/cording foot (optional)

✓ Darning/stippling foot

✓ Fabric stabilizer

✓ Wooden embroidery hoop

✓ Bobbinfill

✓ Basic sewing kit (see p. 8)

DECORATIVE TOP STITCHING

Top stitching shows on the right side of the work so, although you can quickly stitch up a hem with a straight stitch, you can also use top stitching purely for its decorative effect, creating interest with contrast colour, decorative stitches, multiple rows of stitches and twin-needle stitching.

1 Mark the stitching line on the right side of the fabric using a chalk pencil or vanishing pen.

2 Insert a size 12–14 (80–90) needle and thread the machine with a decorative machine thread. The thread could be in a contrast colour, have a metallic finish or, for really pronounced stitching, be buttonhole weight.

3 Select straight stitch or a suitable decorative stitch with a length of 3–3.5. Try out the stitches and their positioning, using a sample of the project fabric with the same number of layers and interfacings. Experiment to see how the stitches look at the corners or around curves; it might be better to pivot with the needle on the inner, or on the outer, side of the corner or curve.

4 When sewing multiple rows, stitch them all in the same direction, using the edge of the presser foot as a guide.

EXPERT TIP
USE THE EDGE OF THE PRESSER FOOT AS A GUIDE FOR LINING UP STITCHING WITH THE EDGE OF THE FABRIC OR WITH OTHER ROWS OF STITCHES.

COUCHING

Couching (also known as gimping) is a way of adding textural detail by zigzag stitching over a decorative thread or trim laid on the surface of the cloth. All sorts of trim, including cords, ribbons and yarns, can be couched in place and your choice will determine the most suitable zigzag stitch and top thread to use. For example, you could completely conceal a plain cord with close zigzag (satin) stitch to create a raised design in a contrast colour. However, if you choose to couch a pretty yarn, you can allow it to be the main focus of attention by using invisible or the same colour of thread with a zigzag that is hardly visible.

1 Mark the stitching line for your design on the right side of the fabric using a chalk pencil or vanishing pen. Pin the trim in place. Select a zigzag stitch to suit the yarn, for example, close satin stitch to cover plain cord, wide three-step zigzag stitch to hold flat ribbon in place or regular zigzag stitch for bulky yarn.

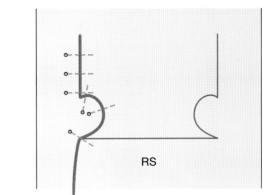

FIGURE 1 PIN THE CORD ALONG THE DESIGN LINE.

2 Place the work under the presser foot so that the needle will go down close to the left of the trim. Turn the balance wheel by hand to work one or two stitches slowly and check that they are long enough to go just over the trim without catching it. Increase or reduce the stitch length as necessary.

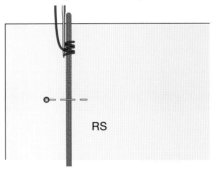

FIGURE 2 CHECK THAT THE STITCHES ARE NOT TOO LONG OR TOO SHORT.

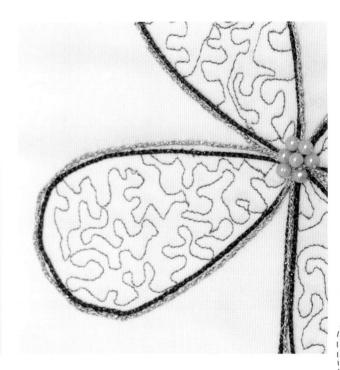

3 Continue stitching over the trim, slowing down at curves and corners. When going around an outer curve, stop with the needle down in the right-hand position, raise the foot to pivot the work slightly, lower the foot and continue. On inner curves, stop with the needle down in the left-hand position.

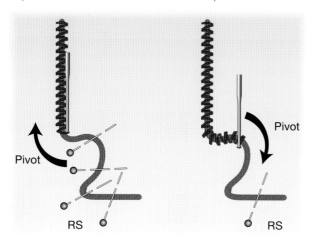

FIGURE 3   TO SEW SMOOTHLY AROUND CURVES AND CORNERS. PIVOT THE WORK AROUND THE NEEDLE.

EXPERT TIP
A CORDING FOOT IS AVAILABLE FOR MOST SEWING MACHINES. IT HAS GROOVES IN THE BASE OF THE FOOT THROUGH WHICH THE CORD FLOWS. MAKING IT EASIER TO GUIDE THE CORD AS YOU SEW AND UNNECESSARY TO PIN IT IN PLACE FIRST.

FREE-MOTION STITCHING
Also known as free-style stitching, this is a way of 'painting with thread' because you control the length and spacing of the stitches by moving the fabric faster or slower in any direction you want. To do this, you will need to drop the feed dogs on the machine and use a darning foot, both to allow free movement across the fabric.

LOWERING THE FEED DOGS
The feed dogs are the little gripper teeth that come up from below the throat plate on the machine. When raised, they help to feed the fabric as it is stitched. When lowered, they disengage and do not come into contact with the fabric.

For free-motion stitching, lower the feed dogs using the appropriate lever or dial on your machine. It is usually found under the accessory table, but check the instruction manual. On older machines or more basic models, it may be necessary to cover the feed dogs rather than lower them. There may be a plate for this purpose or you could tape a piece of thin card over them. Reduce the stitch length to 0.

USING A DARNING FOOT
For free-motion stitching, it is helpful to use a darning/stippling foot, which doesn't sit on the fabric and therefore allows freedom of movement. This special foot has a large, usually oval-shaped hole, through which the needle can swing sideways for wide zigzag stitch, as well as straight stitch.

It is possible to stitch without a presser foot at all, although it is necessary to lower the presser foot lever in order to engage the tension on the top thread. As the aim is to be able to move the fabric in any direction at will, it may also be necessary to release the pressure on the presser foot and you should check your instruction manual for how to do this.

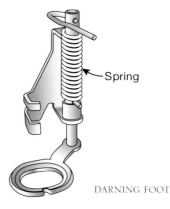

DARNING FOOT

USING AN EMBROIDERY HOOP
To prevent the fabric puckering and distorting while being stitched, hold it taut in an embroidery hoop. Available from most needlework stores, wooden or spring hoops have two rings, the outer one with a screw for tightening.

Lay the stabilized fabric, right side up, over the outer ring. Insert the inner ring inside the outer one, gripping the fabric around the edges. Tighten the rings by turning the screw on the outer ring, pulling the fabric so it is drum-tight.

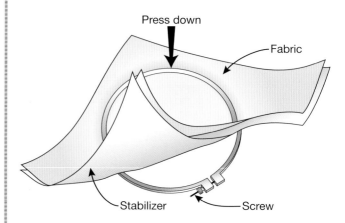

FIGURE 4   PRESS THE INNER RING INTO THE OUTER RING. TRAPPING THE FABRIC.

SEWING SENSE

*If using a wooden hoop, wrap one of the
rings with strips of cotton fabric or tape,
which will help it to grip the fabric.*

GETTING THE RIGHT TENSION

For regular sewing, the top and bobbin tensions need to be
balanced to make perfect stitches. With free-motion embroidery
you can alter the tension to create different textures and effects.

It is easiest to alter the top tension, which can be increased or
decreased to change the texture of the stitches. If you want the
bobbin thread to show on the surface of the work, for example
for shading and texture, tighten the top tension by turning the
dial to a higher number.

Altering the bobbin tension usually requires turning a screw
on the bobbin case. To increase the amount of bobbin thread
showing on the surface of the work, loosen the bobbin screw
a little. To prevent the bobbin thread showing on the surface,
tighten the tension to restrict the flow of the bobbin thread.

SEWING SENSE

*To see the effects of altering the tension, use
different colours for bobbin and top thread.*

EXPERT TIP

IT CAN BE DIFFICULT TO RETURN THE BOBBIN
TENSION TO THE OPTIMUM SETTING FOR REGULAR
STITCHING, SO KEEP A SEPARATE BOBBIN CASE FOR
FREE-MOTION, CREATIVE STITCHING.

STARTING TO STITCH

SEWING SENSE

*Before beginning any free-motion stitching,
experiment on scrap fabric to check that
tensions are correct for the sort of stitched
effect you desire.*

1 Set the stitch width and length to 0. Attach a darning/stippling
foot and release the pressure on the presser foot.

2 Back the fabric with stabilizer and then put it in a hoop. Place
the hoop under the needle so that the fabric lays right side up
and flat on the machine bed.

EXPERT TIP

IF AN EMBROIDERY HOOP AND A FABRIC STABILIZER
ARE NOT AVAILABLE, PLACE ONE OR TWO LAYERS
OF WRITING PAPER UNDER THE WORK TO PROVIDE
STABILITY. RIP THE PAPER AWAY WHEN THE STITCHING
IS COMPLETE.

3 Lower the presser foot to engage the top tension and then use
the balance wheel to lower and raise the needle once, bringing
up the bobbin thread. Hold both thread tails in your left hand and
take two or three stitches over the tails to secure them. Trim the
thread tails.

4 Gently hold the hoop, keeping your fingers away from the
needle, and move it backwards and forwards as you press
down on the foot pedal for a steady medium speed. As you gain
confidence, you can vary the length of the stitches; the quicker
you move the hoop, the larger the stitches, the slower and
smaller the movement, the smaller the stitch. You can move the
hoop in any direction from small circular movements to spiralling
circles or large vertical movements to create long stitches that
look like grasses.

SEWING SENSE

*If possible, set the sewing machine to stitch
slowly so you can control the movement
more easily.*
*If you wish, mark out a design idea using a
vanishing pen or chalk pencil.*

FILLING USING ZIGZAG STITCH

You can fill areas in quickly using zigzag stitch with free motion.
Select zigzag stitch and increase the stitch width to make wider
blocks, decreasing it to zero to make small raised dots. Move the
hoop forwards and backwards to fill the area.

FILLING WITH STIPPLING STITCH

Many modern machines offer a stippling stitch – a random-
looking curvy three-step zigzag. It is very useful for filling open
areas of patchwork, anchoring the layers together. Alternatively,
create a stipple effect by dropping the feed dogs, using a darning
presser foot and selecting 0 stitch length, so you can control the
movement and stitch length.

handsome HEADBOARD

A PLAIN COTTON FABRIC LOOKS FABULOUS DECORATED WITH COUCHED THREADS, FREE-HAND MACHINE EMBROIDERY AND FLANGED CORD. THIS FOAM BLOCK HEADBOARD IS FIXED TO THE WALL WITH WOODEN BATONS AND HOOK AND LOOP TAPE.

YOU WILL NEED
For a single bed:

✓ 1½yd (1.4m) x 60in-wide (150cm-wide) plain fabric

✓ 1⅛yd (1m) x ½in-thick (1.25cm-thick) batting

✓ 2 reels of machine embroidery thread (to match yarn below)

✓ 1 reel of bobbinfill

✓ 2 balls of crochet yarn, or similar, in two colours

✓ 35 beads and beading needle

✓ 3½yd (3m) flanged cord

✓ Paper or card to make patterns

✓ Embroidery hoop (optional)

✓ Darning foot

✓ Cording foot (optional)

✓ Zipper/piping foot

✓ 36 x 22 x 3in (90 x 56 x 7.5cm) block of foam

✓ 1 reel of matching general-purpose sewing thread

✓ 2yd (2m) of hook and loop tape

✓ 2 x 36in-long (90cm-long) wooden battens and wall fixings

✓ Staple gun

✓ Basic sewing kit (see p. 8)

TECHNICAL KNOW-HOW
Free-motion machine embroidery (see p. 94–95)
Stipple stitching (see p. 95)
Couching (see p. 93)
Attaching flanged cord (see pp. 77–79)

CUTTING OUT THE FABRIC

1 Cut the following pieces of fabric. Note that the front panel is slightly larger than the back panel to allow for the foam and batting.

- 1 front panel: 40 x 26in (100 x 66cm)
- 1 back panel: 37¼ x 23¼in (94.5 x 59cm)
- 2 side panels: 23¼ x 4in (59 x 10cm)
- 2 panels for the top and bottom: 37¼ x 4in (94.5 x 10cm)

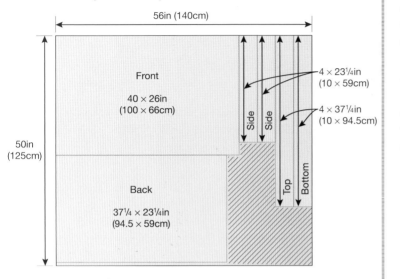

FIGURE 1 CUT OUT THE SIX FABRIC PANELS FROM 60IN-WIDE (150CM-WIDE) FABRIC.

2 Cut one piece of batting the same size as the front panel.

EMBELLISHING THE FRONT PANEL

1 Place the front panel face down on a flat surface and smooth it out. Lay the batting on top. Pin the two layers together around the outer edges and baste them together.

2 Make five flower patterns from the template on p. 142. Arrange them on the right side of the front panel. When you are happy with the positioning, mark the petal outlines with a vanishing pen. Then mark in the stem lines.

FIGURE 2 MARK THE OUTLINES OF THE DESIGN ON THE FABRIC.

3 Pin through the fabric and batting in the centre of each flower shape and along the stems to keep the layers together while stitching. Remove the pins later as the work progresses.

4 Put the first flower shape into the embroidery hoop (see pp. 94–95), unless you prefer to stitch without one. Thread the machine with machine embroidery thread and the bobbin with bobbinfill. Drop the feed dogs, fit a darning foot and set the stitch length and width to 0.

5 Sew with stippling stitch inside the marked petal areas, moving the fabric or hoop smoothly and steadily (see p. 95). Re-hoop and stipple stitch the petals of the remaining flower shapes.

FIGURE 3 STIPPLE STITCH INSIDE THE PETAL OUTLINES.

6 Raise the feed dogs when the stippling stitch is complete and before continuing any more stitching.

7 Prepare the sewing machine to couch the yarn in place for the petal outlines and stems. Fit a cording foot, if available. Thread the machine with machine embroidery thread to match the first couching yarn, keeping bobbinfill in the bobbin. Set the machine to zigzag stitch, with the width and length to suit the thickness of the couching yarn.

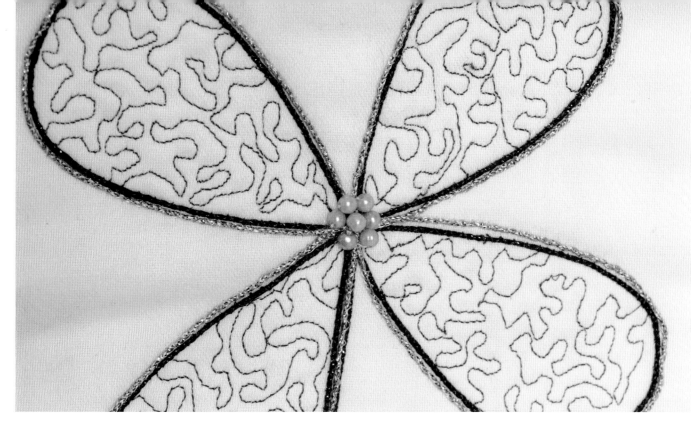

8 For each flower, start couching the yarn at the bottom end of the stem, working up the stem and then around the petals taking the yarn across the centre after each petal and without cutting it until you finish at the centre (see p. 93 for couching techniques). Trim the threads and yarn.

9 Change the top thread to match the second couching yarn. Couch that yarn around the petals close to the first, taking care not to stitch through the yarn. Trim the threads and yarn.

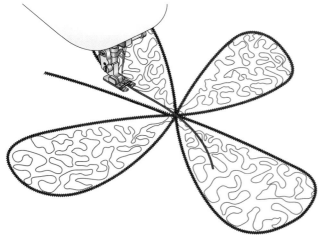

FIGURE 4 COUCH THE YARN IN ONE CONTINUOUS LENGTH, UP THE STEM AND AROUND EACH PETAL.

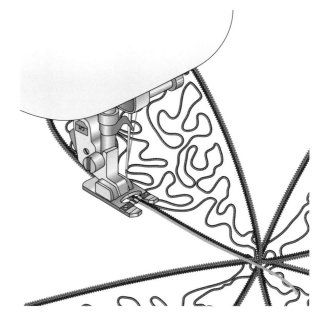

FIGURE 5 COUCH DOWN THE SECOND YARN, TAKING CARE NOT TO STITCH INTO EITHER YARN.

SEWING SENSE

Instead of using a colour of thread to match each couched yarn, you could use invisible thread and couch both yarns at once.

EXPERT TIP

AS AN ALTERNATIVE TO A CORDING FOOT, USE AN OPEN TOE FOOT AND A POINTING TOOL (SUCH AS A CLOSED PAIR OF EMBROIDERY SCISSORS) TO HELP DIRECT THE CORD. THIS REQUIRES MORE CONTROL BUT VISIBILITY IS MUCH BETTER.

10 To complete the embellishment, sew seven beads to the centre of each flower. Use a fine beading needle and double thread, finishing the thread ends securely on the wrong side.

COMPLETE EACH FLOWER WITH BEADS.

MAKING THE HEADBOARD

1 Place the front panel centrally, wrong side down, over the block of foam. Pin through the front panel to mark a seam line around all the edges of the foam. Trim the seam allowance to ⅝in (1.5cm) outside the pin line.

FIGURE 7   MARK THE SEAM LINE WITH PINS AND TRIM THE SEAM ALLOWANCE TO ⅝IN (1.5CM).

2 Pin the flanged cord around the seam line, starting in the centre along the bottom, working up one side of the front panel, across the top and down the other side, and finishing at the start point. Clip into the flange to allow it to turn smoothly and sit flat around the 90-degree corners. Baste the flange if necessary.

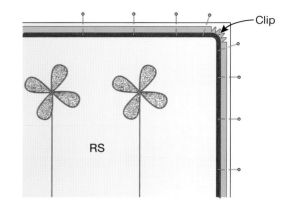

FIGURE 8   PIN THE FLANGED CORD IN PLACE, CLIPPING THE FLANGE AROUND THE CORNERS.

EXPERT TIP

SEW THE FLANGED CORD IN PLACE WITH MACHINE BASTING FIRST. THIS DOES NOT NEED TO BE CLOSE TO THE CORD, JUST HOLDING THE FLANGE IN THE CORRECT POSITION TO MAKE IT EASIER TO SEW CLOSE TO THE CORD AT THE NEXT STAGE.

3 Fit a piping or zipper foot to the sewing machine and sew the flange cord in place.

4 Sew one side panel to the top panel along one short end, right sides together and taking a ⅝in (1.5cm) seam allowance. Repeat to join the other side panel and the bottom panel. Then sew the joined panels together.

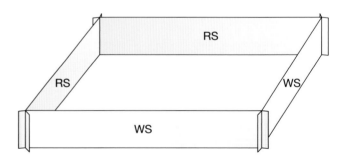

FIGURE 9   JOIN THE TOP, BOTTOM AND SIDE PANELS TOGETHER.

5 With right sides together, pin the side panels to the front panel, matching the corners accurately and trapping the flange in the seam. Working with the front panel uppermost so you can see the basting stitches and position of the cord, sew the panels together as close as possible to the cord.

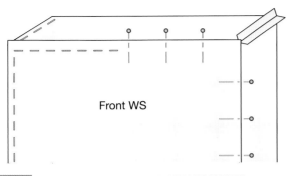

FIGURE 10 PIN AND THEN SEW THE PANELS TOGETHER.

6 Press the seam allowances away from the front panel. Trim and layer the raw edges of the seam allowance to reduce unnecessary bulk.

7 Lay the back panel, right side up, on a flat surface. Mark two centred and parallel 34in (86.5cm) lines across it, 1½in (4cm) from the top and bottom edges. Cut the hook and loop tape into two 34in (86.5cm) lengths. Leave the loop halves of the tape to one side for later. Pin the hook halves along the marked lines on the back panel. Sew around all the edges of the tape and neaten the thread ends securely.

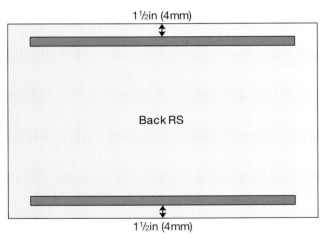

1½in (4mm)

Back RS

1½in (4mm)

FIGURE 11 SEW TWO STRIPS OF HOOK TAPE TO THE RIGHT SIDE OF THE BACK PANEL.

8 Pin the back panel to the narrow side panels, matching up the corners and with right sides together. Sew the panels together with a ⅝in (1.5cm) seam allowance, leaving the bottom edge open. Press the raw edges towards the back panel. Trim and layer the seam allowances of the three seams sewn. Turn the cover right sides out.

9 Insert the foam block, smoothing the cover over it. Tuck in the raw edges of the opening and slip stitch it closed with a double thread.

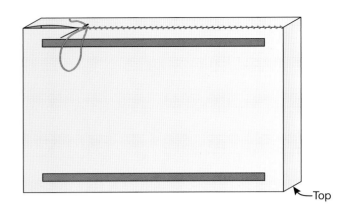

Top

FIGURE 12 SLIP STITCH THE OPENING ALONG THE BACK BOTTOM EDGE CLOSED.

10 Mark the positions on the wall required for the battens, which need to match up with the hook and look tape on the headboard. Fix the battens. Position each strip of hook tape along a batten and, even if the tape is adhesive, secure it with the staple gun.

MORE DESIGN IDEAS

- Add ties or a gathered casing so the headboard can be hung from a curtain pole above the bed.
- Use stitch and stick hook and loop tape to attach the headboard to a plain bed end to create a more traditional padded look.
- Choose a patterned fabric and use machine embroidery techniques to embellish some of the dominant shapes.

MAKING PLEATS

KNIFE-EDGE, INVERTED AND BOX PLEATS ALL ADD DEPTH AND STYLISH DETAIL TO PROJECTS. THE FOLDS MAKING THE PLEATS ALSO CONTROL THE FULLNESS OF THE FABRIC AND CAN BE SOFT OR CRISP, DEPENDING ON THE TYPE OF FABRIC AND THE WAY IT IS PRESSED. PLEATS ARE OFTEN USED THE SKIRTS OF CHAIR COVERS, BED VALANCES AND LAMPSHADES, AS WELL AS ON THE BASE OF POCKETS TO PROVIDE MORE SPACE FOR STORAGE.

IN THE PROJECT ON PP. 106—111, INVERTED PLEATS GIVE A TAILORED LOOK TO THE BEDSPREAD AND KNIFE-EDGE PLEATS ARE ADAPTED TO PROVIDE VERY USEFUL STORAGE IN SIDE POCKETS.

TOOLS AND EQUIPMENT

✓ Cardboard

✓ Pressing cloth

✓ Sheet of parcel paper (optional)

✓ Basic sewing kit (see p. 8)

PLEATING CHOICES

• Inverted pleats are particularly suitable for outside corners as on the skirt of a bedspread or valance.

• Knife-edge pleats and box pleats can be used in a wider range of situations for decorative detail or to add fullness to pockets, for example.

SEWING SENSE

Make sure you measure and form all pleats accurately. An error of just $\frac{1}{8}$in (3mm) on each pleat could mean a surplus or shortage of $1\frac{3}{4}$in (4.5cm) on a piece of fabric with 12 pleats.

MAKING KNIFE-EDGE PLEATS

The knife-edge, or straight, pleat, where all the folds face in the same direction, is the most commonly used.

1 Allow extra fabric across the width to make the depth and number of pleats required. The pleat depth is the total width of fabric needed to form one pleat, which is equal to three times the width of the finished pleat. For instance, a 2in-wide (5cm-wide) finished pleat will have a total depth of 6in (15cm).

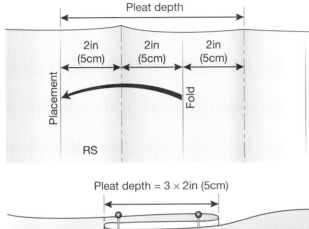

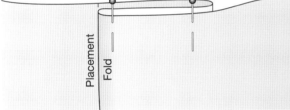

FIGURE 1 CALCULATE THE FABRIC NEEDED FOR EACH PLEAT BY MULTIPLYING THE WIDTH OF THE FINISHED PLEAT BY 3.

2 If you are making pleats on the skirt of a valance or chair cover, first hem the fabric to be pleated.

3 If you want to make a series of uniform pleats, first make a cardboard template to ensure all the pleats are evenly marked and spaced. Cut the template to the depth of the pleat and mark one side 'Fold' and the other 'Placement', depending on whether the pleats are to fold to the left or the right. Mark the fabric, on the wrong side, at the top and bottom of the first pleat. Remember the pleats will fold in the opposite direction on the right side. Repeat across the width of the fabric, carefully measuring even spaces between pleats and marking all the pleats required.

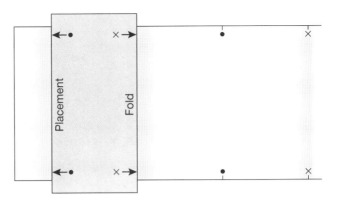

FIGURE 2 USE THE TEMPLATE TO MARK UNIFORM PLEATS.

EXPERT TIP

MARK THE FOLD AND PLACEMENT LINES WITH DIFFERENT COLOURED PINS, MARKERS OR THREAD FOR EASY IDENTIFICATION.

4 To form a pleat, fold the fabric along the fold line and bring that to the placement line. Note that another fold will also be formed in the under-layer of fabric. Match the upper raw edges and pin the pleat in place through all three layers to both folds. If the pleats are to be soft and drop out at the bottom, pin them just along the top edge. If the fabric should hold the pleats to the hem, pin them along the top and bottom. Repeat for the rest of the pleats.

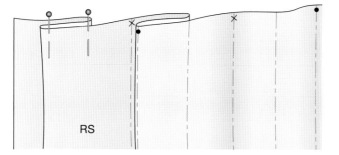

FIGURE 3 PIN EACH PLEAT CLOSE TO BOTH FOLDS.

EXPERT TIP

TO ENSURE PLEATS HANG STRAIGHT, KEEP THE UPPER EDGES EVEN.

5 Press the pleats, either just along the top edge or from top to bottom, depending on how you want them to hold or soften. Press each pleat individually: always use a pressing cloth (or a piece of the project fabric) and, if possible, place a sheet of parcel paper between the pleat and the main fabric to avoid ridges or indentations being formed on the surface fabric.

SEWING SENSE

Always use a press cloth when pressing pleats to avoid leaving imprints of the folds on the fabric.

MAKING INVERTED PLEATS

An inverted pleat consists of two pleats folded towards each other, meeting at the top and forming a recessed inset behind them. The inset part of the pleat can be made from the main fabric or be replaced with a contrast fabric.

1 Make a template and mark the fabric in similar way as for knife-edge pleats, this time on the right side of the fabric. Remember that the placement line is the centre line of the pleat, so flip the template on this line to find the two outer fold lines.

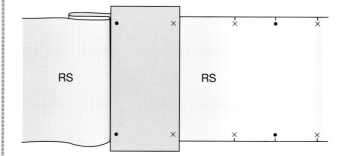

FIGURE 4 FLIP THE TEMPLATE ON THE PLACEMENT LINE TO GIVE THE TWO FOLD LINES FOR AN INVERTED PLEAT.

2 Fold two pleats towards each other to meet in the centre and pin in place. Fold and pin the rest of the pleats. Press the pleats as for knife-edge pleats.

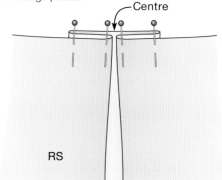

FIGURE 5 PIN THE TWO PLEATS SO THAT THE FOLDS MEET IN THE CENTRE.

EXPERT TIPS

TO HELP PLEATS STAY IN PLACE, STITCH THE TWO LAYERS OF THE INNER FOLD TOGETHER, CLOSE TO THE FOLDED EDGE, ON THE WRONG SIDE.

FOR GREATER DEFINITION, STITCH ALONG THE ENTIRE LENGTH OF THE OUTER FOLD OF THE PLEAT, ON THE RIGHT SIDE OF THE WORK.

INSERTING CONTRAST FABRIC

1 Mark the two inner fold lines of the pleat from top to bottom. Open out the pleat and cut along the marked lines.

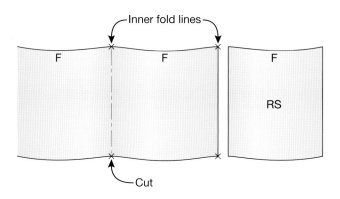

FIGURE 6 CUT ALONG BOTH INNER FOLD LINES.

2 Measure the removed strip and cut another strip in contrast fabric, adding ½in (1.3cm) to both side edges.

3 With right sides together and taking ¼in (6mm) seam allowance, sew the new strip to the side edges of the main pleat. Refold the pleat. Note the seams of the new inset will be very slightly off the fold line, thus reducing the bulk.

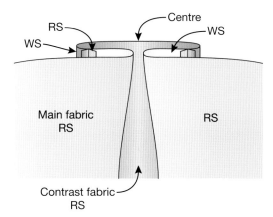

FIGURE 7 REFOLD THE PLEAT SO THE CONTRAST IS INSIDE.

MAKING BOX PLEATS

A box pleat also has two pleats. It is constructed in a similar way to an inverted pleat, but the two component pleats are turned away from each other so there is a flat panel in the centre. In fact, box pleats look like the reverse of inverted pleats.

1 Because the flat panel in the centre of a box pleat is the main feature, first decide on the best position for the flat panel in relation to any pattern on the fabric.

2 Mark two pleats, one on each side on the flat panel, both the same distance from the centre point. Then mark the corresponding placement lines.

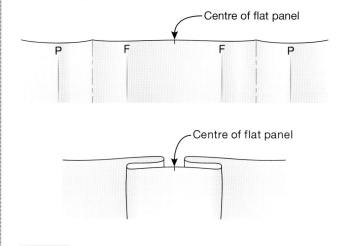

FIGURE 8 MARK THE FOLD AND PLACEMENT LINES, WORKING OUT FROM THE CENTRE OF THE FLAT PANEL.

3 Fold and turn the pleats outwards from the flat panel so that they meet in the centre and pin them in place. Fold and pin the rest of the pleats. Press the pleats as for knife-edge pleats.

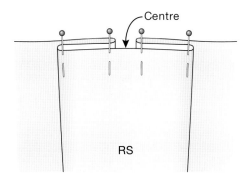

FIGURE 9 PIN THE TWO PLEATS SO THAT THE FOLDS MEET IN THE CENTRE.

beautiful TAILORED BEDSPREAD

THIS VERY SMART BEDSPREAD WAS MADE FROM READY-TRIMMED FABRIC. IT HAS AN INVERTED PLEAT AT EACH CORNER AND AN OPTIONAL SIDE POCKET FOR STORING BEDTIME READING AND THE REMOTE CONTROL. WITH ITS COORDINATING PILLOWCASE, IT'S IDEAL FOR A SPARE ROOM OR A STUDIO APARTMENT.

YOU WILL NEED

For a single bed

✓ 4¾yd (4.5m) x 60in-wide (150-cm) lightweight furnishing fabric

✓ 2yd (1.6m) x 36in-wide (90cm) contrast fabric for pocket lining and pillow

✓ Pencil and paper

✓ 10in (25cm) x ¾in-wide (2cm-wide) hook and loop fastener

✓ 2 reels of matching general-purpose sewing thread

✓ Basic sewing kit (see p. 8)

TECHNICAL KNOW-HOW
Making pleats (see pp. 102–105)

FABRIC CALCULATION

The quantity of fabric given in the panel is for a single bed (see the cutting layout for 60in-wide (150cm-wide) fabric on p. 108). To calculate how much you need for another size of bed or to use a different width of fabric, measure the bed, add the allowances (see below) and plan the panels on paper, with the bed length down the length of fabric.

MEASURING THE BED

Take a note of the following measurements for calculating the quantity of fabric needed and for cutting out the panels.

1 For the centre panel: mattress length plus 2in (5cm) x mattress width.

2 For the welt:
• two side welts: mattress length plus 2in (5cm) x mattress depth
• one end welt: mattress width x mattress depth.

3 For the skirt:
• two side skirts: mattress length plus 6in (15cm) x height from the bottom of the mattress to the floor plus 1in (2.5cm)
• one end skirt: mattress width plus 12in (30cm) x height from the bottom of the mattress to the floor plus 1in (2.5cm).

4 Add ⅝in (1.5cm) seam allowances all around each of the panels.

EXPERT TIP

TAKE THE BED MEASUREMENTS OVER THE BED LINEN THAT WILL NORMALLY BE USED TO ENSURE THE BEDSPREAD FITS CORRECTLY.

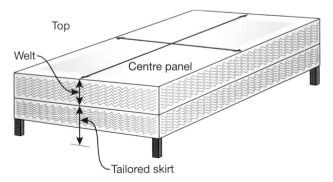

Top

Welt

Centre panel

Tailored skirt

FIGURE 1 MEASURE THE BED, ADDING ALL THE ALLOWANCES IN STEPS 1—4 ABOVE.

CUTTING OUT

Mark out the pieces listed below, using tailor's chalk and a long ruler. Work on the wrong side of the fabric and along the straight grain. Label each piece and mark the edges to be hemmed. Then cut out all the pieces.

MAIN FABRIC

- One centre panel, three welt panels and three skirt panels for the bedspread; to make assembly easier, round off the bottom corners of the centre panel using a saucer and chalk
- 14 x 15in (35.5 x 38cm) for one pocket
- 7 x 18½in (18 x 47cm) for the pillowcase

CONTRAST FABRIC

- 14 x 15in (35.5 x 38cm) for one pocket lining
- 18½in x 64in (47 x 162cm) for the pillowcase

MAKING THE BEDSPREAD

1 With right sides together and taking ⅝in (1.5cm) seam allowances (and throughout the project), join one short edge of each side welt to the short edges of the end welt. Press the seams open.

2 With right sides together, pin and then baste the welt to the centre panel, making sure each welt seam lines up with the centre of a rounded corner. Stitch the welt in place, carefully clipping around the corners so it sits smoothly.

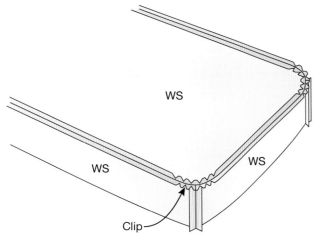

FIGURE 2 SEW THE PIECED WELT TO THE CENTRE PANEL.

3 Join the skirt panels in the same way as the welts. Then neaten the lower edge with a ⅝in (1.5cm) hem. Lay the panels flat, right side uppermost. Using chalk, mark vertical lines 6in (15cm) on either side of the two seams.

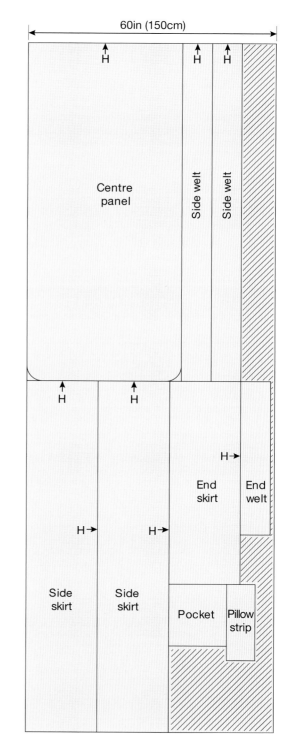

FIGURE 3 USE THIS LAYOUT FOR CUTTING OUT THE MAIN FABRIC PANELS FOR A SINGLE BED FROM 60IN-WIDE (150CM-WIDE) FABRIC. H INDICATES EDGES TO BE HEMMED.

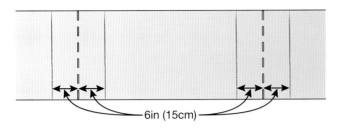

FIGURE 4 MARK THE PLEAT FOLD LINES ON THE SKIRT, 6IN (15CM) FROM THE TWO SEAMS.

4 Make the inverted pleats (see p. 104), pinning the chalked fold lines on top of the seam lines. Press the pleats firmly in place from top to bottom. Baste the top of the pleats to hold them in place.

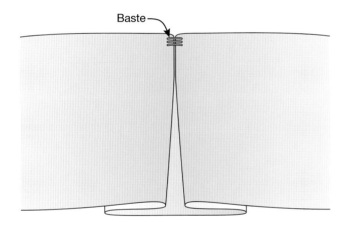

FIGURE 5 BASTE THE TOP OF EACH PLEAT.

5 With right sides together, pin and then baste the skirt to the welt, making sure the centre of each pleat lines up with the corresponding seam on the welt. Sew in place and press.

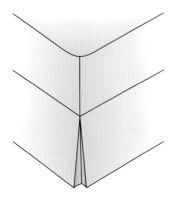

FIGURE 6 LINE UP THE SEAMS ON THE WELT AND THE SKIRT.

6 Finish the bedspread by neatening all the raw edges at the top end with a ⅝in (1.5cm) hem. Press.

MAKING THE POCKET

1 With right sides together, join the pocket and the lining, leaving the lower edge open. Turn the pocket to the right side and press in the turnings on the lower edge.

2 Lay the pocket flat, right side uppermost. Using chalk, mark a vertical line 2in (5cm) in from each side edge. Fold the fabric along the chalk lines and lay each fold on an outside edge of the pocket. Press firmly in place. Edge stitch along the two outer folds to emphasise the pleat.

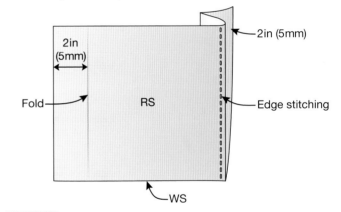

FIGURE 7 CREATE A STITCHED PLEAT ON EACH SIDE OF THE POCKET AND THEN EDGE STITCH THE OUTER FOLDS.

3 Stitch the hook tape to the wrong side of the top edge of the pocket, centred between the pleats.

4 Position the pocket on the bedspread in a convenient position and mark the top edge with chalk. Stitch the loop tape to the bedspread, centred along the chalk line.

5 Pin the pocket to the bedspread, closing the hook and loop tape. Stitch the side edges of the pocket to the bedspread, making sure you do not catch the pleat in the stitching. Then stitch the bottom edge of the pocket, making sure you do catch the pleat in place.

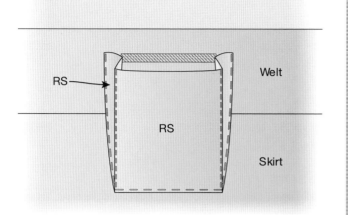

FIGURE 8 FIRST SEW THE POCKET SIDES AND THEN ACROSS THE BOTTOM TO ENSURE THE PLEATS OPEN DOWN THE SIDES BUT ARE FIXED ALONG THE BOTTOM.

RS

Welt

RS

Skirt

MAKING THE PILLOWCASE

1 Turn under the long side edges on the strip of main fabric for the pillowcase. Position the strip on the right side of the contrast fabric, 9in (22.5cm) from one end with the raw edges even. Top stitch along the neatened long edges to attach the strip.

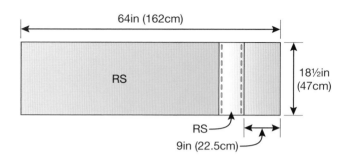

64in (162cm)

RS

18½in (47cm)

RS

9in (22.5cm)

FIGURE 8 TOP STITCH ALONG THE SIDE EDGES OF THE STRIP OF MAIN FABRIC.

2 Neaten each short end of the contrast fabric by turning under ⅜in (1cm) once and then again. Top stitch them in place.

3 Turn under 2in (5cm) to the wrong side on the end nearest the decorative strip. At the opposite end, turn 4½in (11.5cm) to the right side. Press both folds in place.

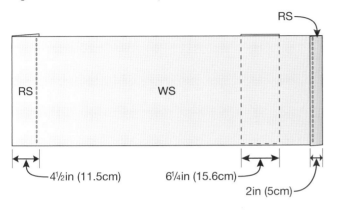

FIGURE 9 TURN THE ENDS TO THE WRONG SIDE.

4 Fold the pillowcase in half, right sides together, tucking the narrow folded end inside the wide folded end. Sew along the top and bottom edges incorporating the folds. Neaten the raw edges and press. Turn the pillowcase right side out and press again. Insert the pillow into the case and tuck it under the wider fold.

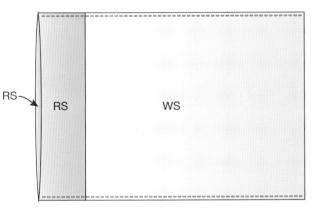

FIGURE 10 SEW ALONG THE TOP AND BOTTOM EDGES.

MORE DESIGN IDEAS

- Make a bedspread with lots of different sized pockets for the teenager who needs to tidy up all their small gadgets.
- Buy extra fabric and make accessories such as cushions, shoe carriers and padded hangers to give your room a totally coordinated look.
- Use two fabrics to make the bedspread centre panel and skirt in one and the welt and pillowcase in the other.

SEWING SPECIAL SEAMS

SOMETIMES A STRAIGHT STITCH SEAM IS NOT TOTALLY SUITABLE FOR THE PROJECT IN HAND — FOR EXAMPLE, IF THE REVERSE IS GOING TO BE VISIBLE, WHERE THE FABRIC IS VERY BULKY OR JUST TO ADD DETAIL. IN SUCH CASES, IT IS USEFUL TO HAVE A REPERTOIRE OF DIFFERENT SEAMS. PARTICULARLY HANDY CHOICES INCLUDE THE TOP-STITCHED SEAM, AS WELL AS FRENCH, LAPPED AND WELT SEAMS.

THE STYLISH LAUNDRY BASKET LINER ON PP. 116—119 MAKES VERY GOOD USE OF FRENCH SEAMS.

SEAM CHOICES

There are three main reasons to choose alternative seams – if the reverse side is clearly visible, if the fabric is particularly bulky or depending on how much the fabric is likely to fray.

- French seams neatly encase raw edges and so are ideal when the reverse or underside of a project is visible, such as when sewing with transparent fabrics or lining a basket.
- Lapped seams suit fabrics that don't fray and are visible from both sides, as on reversible covers.
- Welt seams provide a neat and less bulky finish when sewing thicker, heavyweight fabrics.
- Whichever seam is most suitable, you might also choose to embellish it with top stitching – with simple straight stitches or, more decoratively, with any of the automatic stitches on your sewing machine.

SEWING SENSE
Always press seams before trimming the seam allowance or sewing over them again.

TOOLS AND EQUIPMENT
✓ Basic sewing kit (see p. 8)

SEWING TOP-STITCHED SEAMS

Top stitching (see p. 93) shows on the right side of the fabric. It can be sewn in matching or contrasting thread, using a straight or decorative stitch. Top-stitch thread, which is thicker than regular sewing thread and needs to be threaded through a needle with a larger eye, can also be used to give a more prominent finish. A top-stitched seam is more robust, holds the seam allowances in place on the underside and adds a decorative element.

1 Stitch a straight stitch seam, with right sides together. Press and neaten the seam allowances. On lightweight fabrics, press the seam allowances to one side. For medium- to heavyweight fabrics, press the seam allowances open.

2 Thread the machine with top-stitching thread. If both seam allowances are pressed to the same side, you may need to increase the stitch length slightly so that the stitches look effective sewn through all the layers of fabric. Test stitch on the same number of layers of fabric remnants.

3 Working from the right side, top stitch about ¼in (6mm) from the seam line, stitching down the side that has the seam allowances underneath.

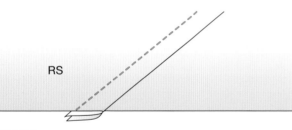

FIGURE 1 TOP STITCH CLOSE TO THE SEAM LINE THROUGH ALL THE LAYERS.

4 For fabrics that have the seam allowances pressed open, stitch on both sides of the seam, about ⅜in (1cm) from the seam line.

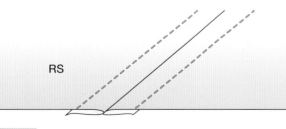

FIGURE 2 TOP STITCH ON BOTH SIDES OF THE SEAM LINE.

SEWING FRENCH SEAMS

This is a particularly neat seam to be used when the reverse side will be visible or the item will get heavy wear or laundering, because it encases all the raw edges. However, it only works really well on a straight seam.

1 With the wrong sides of the fabric together, sew a plain seam ⅜in (1cm) from the edge. Trim the seam allowance to a scant ⅛in (3mm) and press. Turn the fabric so the rights sides are facing and the original seam line is on the fold. Press again.

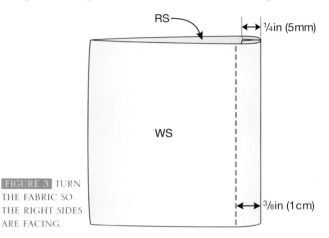

FIGURE 3 TURN THE FABRIC SO THE RIGHT SIDES ARE FACING.

2 Working in the same direction as before, sew a second seam about ¼in (6mm) from the folded edge. Open out the fabric and press the seam to one side.

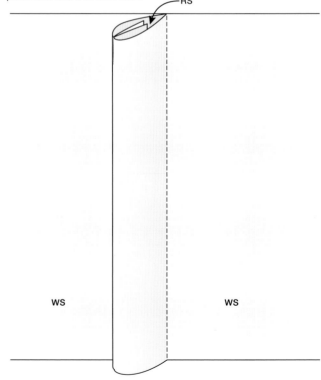

FIGURE 4 ENCASE THE RAW EDGES WITHIN THE FRENCH SEAM.

SEWING LAPPED SEAMS

A lapped seam is useful for thicker fabrics that don't fray or ravel, such as boiled wool, fleece or faux suede. The seam allowances are simply overlapped, without neatening, and stitched in place. Horizontal seams should be lapped downwards and vertical seams lapped away from the centre.

1 Mark the stitching line on both pieces of fabric. Trim off the seam allowance on one of the pieces.

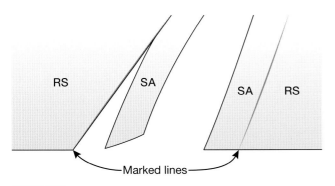

FIGURE 5 TRIM THE SEAM ALLOWANCE FROM ONE PIECE OF THE FABRIC.

2 Lay the trimmed fabric over the other piece, so the trimmed edge is just over the marked seam line on the underlying fabric. Edge stitch very close to the trimmed edge. Then, in the same direction, top stitch ¼in (6mm) from the first row of stitching, securing the remaining seam allowance.

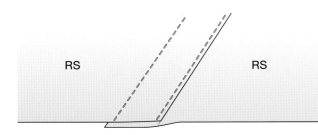

FIGURE 6 EDGE STITCH AND TOP STITCH THE SEAM.

EXPERT TIP

IF WORKING WITH FABRIC THAT MAY BE MARKED BY PINS, USE DOUBLE-SIDED BASTING TAPE TO HOLD THE LAYERS TOGETHER.

SEWING WELT AND DOUBLE WELT SEAMS

These seams are particularly suitable for heavyweight and bulky fabrics. They involve top stitching, but bulk is reduced in the seam allowance.

1 Stitch a straight stitch seam in the usual way. Trim one seam allowance to ¼in (6mm). Press both seam allowances to one side, with the wider one on the top.

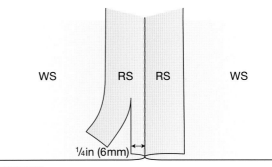

FIGURE 7 TRIM ONE SEAM ALLOWANCE.

2 Turn the work to the right side and top stitch ¼in (6mm) from the seam line, stitching the wider seam allowance in place and encasing the trimmed one.

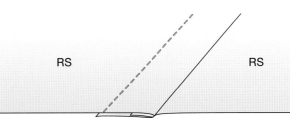

FIGURE 8 TOP STITCH ¼IN (6MM) FROM THE SEAM LINE.

3 Add an additional row of top stitching very close to the seam line for a double welt seam.

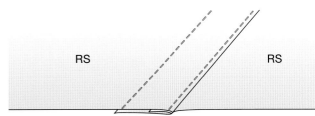

FIGURE 9 TOP STITCH VERY CLOSE TO THE SEAM LINE.

LAUNDRY BASKET LINER

KEEP YOUR LINEN SAFE FROM SNAGS
BY MAKING THIS STYLISH LINER FOR
YOUR LAUNDRY BASKET. YOU CAN
ALSO LIFT THE LINER OUT OF THE
BASKET TO CARRY YOUR LAUNDRY
TO THE WASHING MACHINE QUICKLY
AND EASILY IN ONE LOAD. COTTON,
LINEN OR CALICO FABRIC ARE GOOD
CHOICES SO YOU CAN WASH THE
LINER AS WELL.

SEWING SENSE
*Wash new fabric before using it to eliminate
any unwanted shrinkage later on.*

FABRIC CALCULATIONS

1 For the liner sides panel:
- depth: measure the height of the basket and add 8in (20cm)
- width : measure the circumference of the basket and add 1¼in (3cm) for seam allowances.

2 For the liner base, measure the base of the basket and add ⅝ in (1.5cm) all around for seam allowances.

3 To calculate the total length of fabric required, add the depth of the liner base to the depth of the liner.

YOU WILL NEED

✓ Light- or medium-weight 54in-wide (135cm-wide) fabric (as calculated above)

✓ 1 reel of matching general-purpose sewing thread

✓ Ribbon or cord: circumference of the basket plus 12in (30cm)

✓ Safety pin

✓ Basic sewing kit (see p. 8)

SEWING SENSE
If your basket already has a liner, use it as a pattern. Unpick the seams and cut out pieces to match in your choice of fabric.

TECHNIQUES USED
Sewing French seams (see p. 114)
Making bias binding (see pp. 59–60)

CUTTING OUT

1 Cut one panel for the liner sides and another for the liner base.

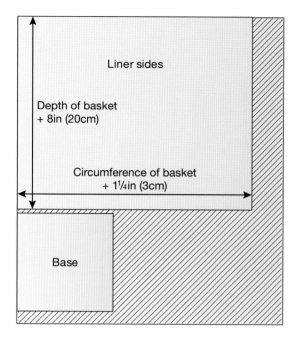

FIGURE 1 CUT OUT THE SIDE PANEL AND THE BASE.

2 Fold the side panel in half, wrong sides together to form a tube. Pin and sew a seam taking a ¼in (5mm) seam allowance. Drop the liner into the basket to check it fits and is the right way up (the base may be larger or smaller than the top). The liner will be taller than the basket.

3 Turn the liner through so the right sides are together and complete the French seam (see p. 114), sewn ⅜in (1cm) from the folded edge. Press.

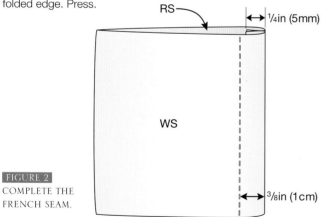

FIGURE 2
COMPLETE THE
FRENCH SEAM.

4 With right sides together, pin the bottom edges of the liner sides to the base. Clip into the seam allowance on the side panel where it meets the corners of the base. Add neat, evenly spaced tucks as necessary to reduce any extra fabric in the side panel to match the base. Sew the side panel to the base. Press the seams towards the base.

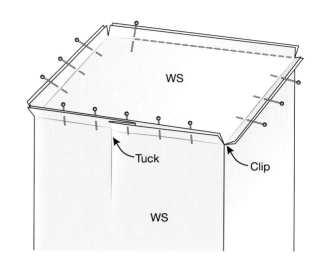

FIGURE 3 MAKE ADJUSTMENTS TO THE SIDE PANEL SO IT ATTACHES TO THE BASE NEATLY.

SEWING SENSE

To prevent the seams from fraying, wrap bias binding around seam allowance and zigzag stitch it in place (see Making bias binding, pp. 59–60). Alternatively, simply zigzag the seam allowances.

5 Zigzag the top edge of the liner to stop it fraying. Fold it down by 3½in (9cm) to the wrong side.

6 Sew the folded top edge to the liner close to the neatened edge to make a casing. Reverse stitch at the start and finish, but leave a ¾in (2cm) opening ready for the ribbon tie. Measure and mark a second stitch line, the width of the ribbon plus ⅜in (1cm) for ease, up from the first row. Sew the second row of stitching all the way around the liner.

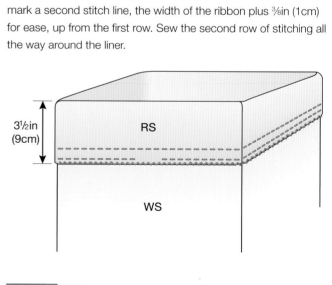

FIGURE 4 FOLD THE TOP EDGE DOWN AND SEW A CASING AROUND THE LINER.

7 Cut the ribbon to length, allowing 12in (30cm) more than the length of the casing. Thread the ribbon through the channel with a safety pin. At the opposite side from the opening, stitch across the ribbon or cord to prevent it from being pulled out.

8 Place the liner in the basket. It should fit snugly, folded over the top edge with the pattern of the fabric showing. When it is full of laundry, remove the liner from the basket and pull the ribbon to gather up the bag.

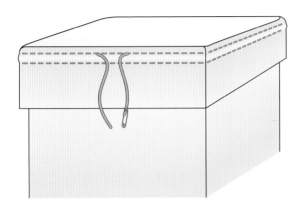

FIGURE 5 PLACE THE LINER IN THE BASKET.

MORE DESIGN IDEAS

• If you have a shabby old basket, make a cover that hides the outside completely. Finish the casing with elastic for a firmer hold at the top.

• Make matching liners for a set of small baskets and boxes for your bathroom or wardrobe.

• If you don't have a linen basket, use this project as a bag, adding a hanging loop to the top to hang it on a door or hook.

WORKING WITH PATTERNED FABRIC

ONE OF THE BEST THINGS ABOUT MAKING SLIPCOVERS YOURSELF IS THAT YOU CAN REALLY TRANSFORM THE LOOK OF THE ROOM BY INTRODUCING A PATTERNED FABRIC THAT COORDINATES WITH YOUR DÉCOR. PAGES 124—127 SHOW JUST HOW EFFECTIVE A NEW COVER FOR AN ARMCHAIR CAN BE. WORKING WITH A PATTERNED FABRIC PRESENTS SOME CHALLENGES, SO BEFORE YOU PICK A PRINT, HERE ARE A FEW USEFUL TIPS AND TECHNIQUES.

FABRIC CHOICES

- The trick to making a patterned fabric look fresh and modern is to use it sparingly and team it with simple accessories. For instance, keep the walls plain and you can have boldly patterned fabric – repainting the walls periodically will update the room.
- Think about proportions too. Large floral or geometric designs look great on big furnishings such as large sofas and squashy armchairs. Small prints work best on smaller items such as cushion covers, simple chair covers and laundry basket liners.
- The size of the room also needs to be taken into account. Large bold prints would overwhelm a small room or one with lots of other furniture or ornaments. They work better in uncluttered and spacious rooms that are light and airy.
- If you really love a larger than life print and want it to feature even in a small room, use it sparingly on scatter cushions or for one armchair cover, and keep everything else plain.

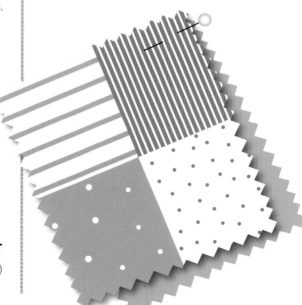

TOOLS AND EQUIPMENT
✓ Basic sewing kit (see p. 8)

FLORAL AND
LEAF PRINTS
ARE TIMELESS
AND PROVIDE A
CLASSIC APPEAL.

STRIPES AND CHECKS
MAKE A BOLD
STATEMENT.
VERTICAL STRIPES
WILL ADD HEIGHT
AND HORIZONTAL
ONES WILL ADD
WIDTH.

YOU CAN PICK OUT ACCENT
COLOURS IN OTHER FURNISHINGS
WITH SPOT-PRINTED FABRIC.

ALLOWING FOR THE PATTERN REPEAT

On larger projects it is often necessary to match the pattern so that it runs across the various panels of fabric. For example, for a large tablecloth, bedspread or box cushion, you might need to piece together at least two widths of fabric. Similarly, if you are making a fitted cover for a sofa, you will want to match the pattern across various panels, including the inner and outer back. To achieve this, you need to make an allowance for the pattern repeat in your calculations to make sure you buy enough fabric and you also need to take it into consideration when cutting the fabric.

The term 'pattern repeat' is used to describe the depth of the pattern that repeats down the length of the fabric and is expressed as a measurement. It is often easiest to measure from the top of a dominant motif down through the pattern, including any plain fabric between the motifs, to the top of the same motif the next time it occurs directly under the first.

SEWING SENSE
The pattern repeat is usually given on the fabric bolt or on the back of a sample. If you are not sure, ask the store assistant to confirm the measurement for you.

FIGURE 1
TO FIND THE PATTERN REPEAT, MEASURE FROM THE TOP OF ONE MOTIF TO THE TOP OF THE SAME MOTIF DIRECTLY BELOW.

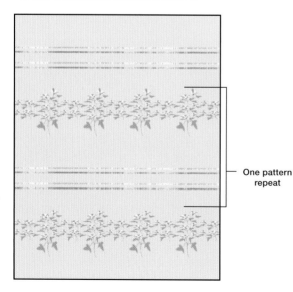

One pattern repeat

POSITIONING A DOMINANT PATTERN

If the fabric you have chosen has a very striking pattern and you have plenty fabric, it is a good idea to decide where you want the most dominant motifs to fall, because they catch the eye most easily. For example, if the pattern has a clear linear element, this certainly needs to run parallel or at right angles to straight edges on the project, and you could plan for it to run along a hemmed edge. Alternatively, if the pattern has striking motifs, these will look best centred on large panels so that, on an armchair for example, the dominant pattern would be centred on the inner back, and run forward across the seat and down the front border, also matching on the fronts of the arms, around the outer arms and across the outer back. Such matching needs careful planning and cutting, but is worth the extra effort to give a really professional finish.

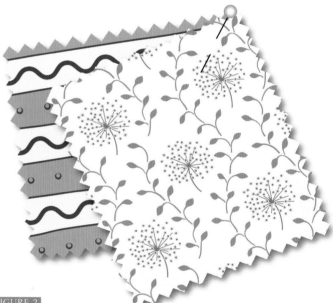

FIGURE 2
THE REPEAT ON AN UNEVEN STRIPE OR SMALL PRINT MIGHT BE 2–4IN (5–10CM). ON A LARGE FLORAL DESIGN, IT MIGHT BE AS MUCH AS 27½IN (70CM).

CALCULATING THE EXTRA REQUIREMENTS

If you need extra fabric to match the pattern repeat across two widths of fabric joined to make one panel, simply add one pattern repeat to the total length of fabric required. However, for a more complex project, such as an armchair, on which lots of panels need to be matched, it is best to plan the shapes out on paper (see p. 129), positioning each panel in relation to the pattern. You will require more fabric if you choose a patterned one, but careful planning will minimise the extra cost.

MATCHING THE PATTERN

1 If necessary, square the top edge of the fabric (see p. 27). With the right side uppermost, cut the first panel to the measurement including any allowances but not the pattern repeat. Remember to take the positioning of the pattern into account if that is important.

2 Keeping the first panel in position, unroll another length of fabric alongside it, matching the pattern at the side edges so that the pattern continues across. This will probably mean that there is some fabric above as well as below the length of the first panel. Alternatively, if you have less space to work in, place the first panel face down over the remaining fabric, matching the pattern. Check that the pattern matches down the length of both panels.

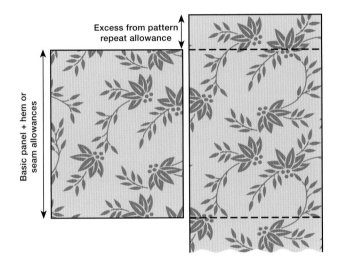

FIGURE 3 MAKE SURE THE PATTERN MATCHES ON BOTH PIECES OF FABRIC BEFORE CUTTING THE SECOND PANEL.

3 Cut the second panel across the top and bottom, using the first panel as a guide. Continue matching and cutting until you have the correct number of panels.

EXPERT TIP
WHEN WORKING ON A PROJECT WITH LOTS OF PIECES TO BE JOINED, CONSIDER CHOOSING A FABRIC WITH A MINIMAL PATTERN REPEAT. IT WILL BE EASIER TO MATCH AND YOU WILL USE LESS FABRIC.

CUTTING HALF PANELS

You may need a half- or even quarter-width panel to make up the total width required. To do this accurately, measure from one side edge to the centre or quarter mark at intervals down the length of the fabric. Draw a chalk line through the marks and then cut the panel.

Main centre panel   Half panel for the outside edges

FIGURE 4 CUT THE HALF-WIDTH PANEL ACCURATELY SO THAT THE PATTERN MATCHES DOWN THE OUTER EDGE OF THE MAIN PANEL.

Always use part panels down the outer edges of a project so that the complete panel is most obvious in the middle and the joins are less apparent.

FIGURE 5 POSITION THE PART PANELS ON THE SIDE EDGES.

SEWING SENSE
While you are cutting the main fabric it makes sense to also cut out any lining. Cut the same number of lining panels as the main fabric, but to the basic measurements (i.e. not including the pattern repeat).

contemporary classic
CHAIR COVER

RESTYLE A FAVOURITE ARMCHAIR WITH
A CONTEMPORARY LOOSE COVER TO
GIVE IT A NEW LEASE OF LIFE. A
COTTON FURNISHING FABRIC IS EASY
TO KEEP CRISP AND CLEAN, AND
STRIPES OR CHECKS MAKE IT SO SIMPLE
TO REPOSITION THE COVER IN EXACTLY
THE RIGHT PLACE EACH TIME.

ALTHOUGH THE METHOD FOR MAKING
THIS SLIP COVER INVOLVES CAREFUL
MEASURING, IT IS SIMPLICITY ITSELF TO
MAKE AND CAN EASILY BE ADAPTED
FOR A SOFA OR SOFABED.

YOU WILL NEED

✓ Light- or medium-weight fabric (as calculated above)
✓ 1 reel of matching general purpose sewing thread
✓ 2yd (2m) ribbon
✓ Safety pins
✓ Basic sewing kit (see p. 8)

EXPERT TIP
AS A VERY ROUGH GUIDE, RECKON ON NEEDING ABOUT 5YD
(4.5M) TO COVER AN ARMCHAIR AND 10YD (9M) TO COVER A
STANDARD-SIZED SOFA.

TECHNICAL KNOW-HOW
Working with patterned fabric (see pp. 122–123)
Finishing seams (see pp. 18–19)

FABRIC CALCULATION

1 For the width needed, measure the chair as shown in Figure 1, making sure you start and finish at floor level and tuck the tape measure down each side of the seat. Add a total of 16in (40cm) for seams and hems.

2 For the length needed, measure the chair as shown in Figure 1, making sure you start and finish at floor level and tuck the tape measure down the back of the seat. Add a total of 16in (40cm) for seams and hems.

3 Work out how many widths of fabric you need. You may need two to cover a chair and three to cover a sofa. Multiply this by the length and add any allowance needed for matching the pattern repeat (see p. 123).

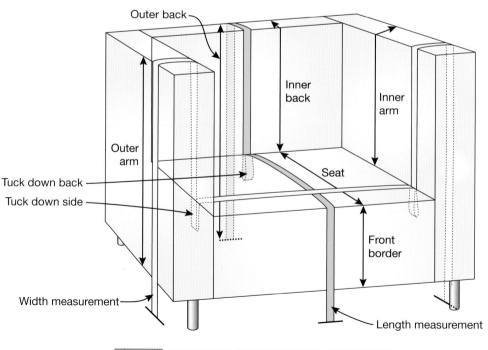

FIGURE 1 MEASURE THE CHAIR TO CALCULATE THE WIDTH AND LENGTH
OF FABRIC NEEDED.

CUTTING OUT

1 Carefully cut to length the number of panels you require.

2 If necessary, cut one panel in half vertically so that the halves can be sewn to each side of the full central panel (see p. 123).

MAKING UP

1 Join the fabric panels as necessary, using a straight stitch and taking a ⅝in (1.5cm) seam allowance. Neaten the raw edges of the seams by overlocking or overcasting (see p. 19) and press.

2 Place the fabric centrally over the chair with the fabric pattern or grain straight and the raw edges hanging on the floor.

3 Mark the centre on the bottom edges at the front and back of the chair with safety pins. Pin the fabric to the top of the seat to stop it moving.

4 Tuck the fabric down the sides of the seat. Check that it still touches the floor below the arms, with surplus to spare, all around. Smooth the fabric to the back of the seat and tuck it down where possible. Check the length at the front and back still touches the floor all around.

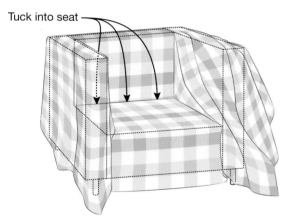

Tuck into seat

FIGURE 2 TUCK THE FABRIC DOWN AROUND THE SEAT, MAKING SURE THERE IS STILL SURPLUS ALL AROUND THE BOTTOM EDGES OF THE CHAIR.

5 Smooth the fabric up the inner back, over the top and down the outer back. Pin it to the top edge of the chair along the outer back.

6 Smooth the fabric over one chair arm, ensuring it is still well tucked down around the seat and keeping the excess of fabric in front of the arm.

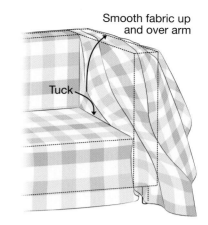

Smooth fabric up and over arm

Tuck

FIGURE 3 KEEP THE EXCESS FABRIC TO THE FRONT OF THE ARM.

7 Run your hand up the inside back corner of the same chair arm to the top of the inner back, tucking the fabric into the corner. Then fold the fabric in at an angle from the inner to the outer back.

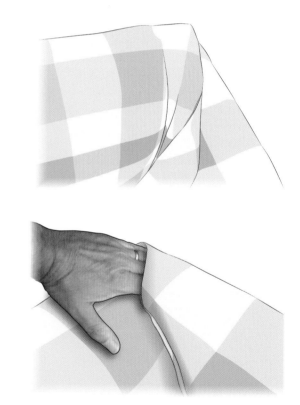

FIGURE 4 FOLD THE FABRIC AT AN ANGLE.

8 Form pleats or folds in the fabric at the front of the arm, draping it to the floor. Mark the positions of the pleats or folds with marker pen. Pin the fabric in place so it does not move.

FIGURE 5 PIN THE PLEATS OR FOLDS IN PLACE AT THE FRONT OF THE ARM.

9 Pin two ½yd (50cm) lengths of ribbon on the outer folds of fabric at a suitable height for the ties. Tie them in place to hold the folds and adjust the fit if necessary.

FIGURE 6 ATTACH AND TIE THE TIES TO CHECK THE FIT.

10 Repeat from step 6 to fit the fabric around the other arm.

11 Now mark the fabric with marker pen or pins where it touches the floor all around the chair. Also mark the back corners of the cover with pins, so that, once removed, you can replace the cover easily on the chair.

12 Untie the ribbons and any pins other than those you need as markers. Carefully remove the cover from the chair.

EXPERT TIP
TAKE A PHOTO OF THE COVER ON THE CHAIR AS A REMINDER OF ITS POSITION.

13 Smooth the cover out on a flat surface a section at a time. Work around the hem edge, adding a ¾in (2cm) seam allowance below the marked line. There will be some curves, but make sure the line is smooth. Cut away the excess fabric.

14 Overlock or zigzag stitch around all the raw edges to prevent fraying. Turn the hem allowance under, easing it around the curves as necessary, and top stitch it in place close to the neatened edge. Machine stitch the ends of the ribbon in place.

15 Replace the cover on the chair, carefully lining the edges up along the floor. Tuck the cover in around the seat and refold the inside corners, making sure the markers are in the correct position. Tie the ribbons and adjust the pleats.

MORE DESIGN IDEAS
• Make different–shaped hems with scallops, castellations or triangles, using a template.
• Cover the seat cushion in a coordinating fabric and place it on top of the loose seat cover.

MAKING SLIP-ON CHAIR COVERS

ONCE YOU'VE MASTERED THE SKILLS FOR MAKING LOOSE COVERS, YOU WILL FEEL CONFIDENT ENOUGH TO MAKE A FITTED SLIP-ON COVER. ACHIEVING A GOOD FIT AND PROFESSIONAL FINISH IS ALL ABOUT CAREFUL MEASURING, CUTTING OUT AND PATTERN FITTING. CHOICES FOR THE TREATMENT AROUND THE BOTTOM EDGE OF THE COVER ARE ALSO EXPLAINED IN THIS SECTION.

MORE DETAILED GUIDANCE ON MAKING UP A CHAIR COVER WITH A SCALLOPED BOTTOM EDGE IS GIVEN IN THE PROJECT ON PP. 134–137.

TOOLS AND EQUIPMENT

✓ Pencil and paper
✓ Pattern or parcel paper
✓ Calico or muslin
✓ Long pins
✓ Hook and loop tape
✓ Basic sewing kit (see p. 8)

COVER CHOICES
- Make the cushion cover in contrasting fabric.
- Insert fringed cord or piping along the top outer edges of the arms and chair back, and around the top and bottom edges of the cushion cover (see pp. 76–79).

TAKING MEASUREMENTS

It is very important to take accurate measurements of the chair before buying any fabric for the cover. In this example, a very basic chair shape is measured for a cover that falls straight to the floor. If you wish to add a separate skirt that goes all around the chair, see p. 132.

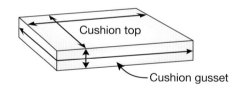

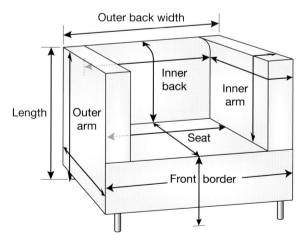

FIGURE 1 MAKE A CAREFUL NOTE OF THE MEASUREMENTS OF EACH SECTION.

1 Take the length and width measurements of the following sections of the chair, as shown on Figure 1:

- outer back: measure the length from the top edge to the floor
- outer arms: measure from the highest part of the arm down to the floor and from the back to the outside edge at the front of the arm
- inner back: measure up from the seat, not from the cushion
- inner arms: measure up from the seat and over the top of the arm to the outside edge and from the inner back around the front of the arm to the outside edge
- seat: measure the length from the back to the front edge and the width from one side to the other
- front border: measure the length from the top front edge of the seat to the floor and the width from the outer edge of one arm to the outer edge of the other arm
- cushion: measure the length and width across the top for the top and bottom panels; also measure from the front left corner round to the back right corner and the height of the cushion for the gusset.

2 Make a clear list of each set of measurements, adding a ¾in (2cm) seam allowance to each edge.

CALCULATING FABRIC REQUIREMENTS

The quickest way to calculate the approximate length of fabric required is to add up the lengths of all the panels. Then add 20in (50cm) extra for adjustment of the layout and more as necessary for the pattern repeat (see pp. 122–123 for Working with pattern repeats).

However, to be more accurate, especially if the fabric is expensive, use the measurements to plan the layout on paper, placing panels side by side across the fabric width and taking any pattern repeat into account.

PREPARING A PATTERN

1 Use the measurements to draw out the pattern pieces as basic rectangles on paper. Label each panel.

2 Using the pattern pieces, cut out the panels in calico, including the seam allowances. Label each panel and mark the back and front or top and bottom edges as appropriate.

3 Pin each panel, right side down, in place on the chair, although not to each other, to check it is big enough. All the seam allowances should overlap by ¾in (2cm).

4 Follow the shape of the chair on each panel and mark the seam lines.

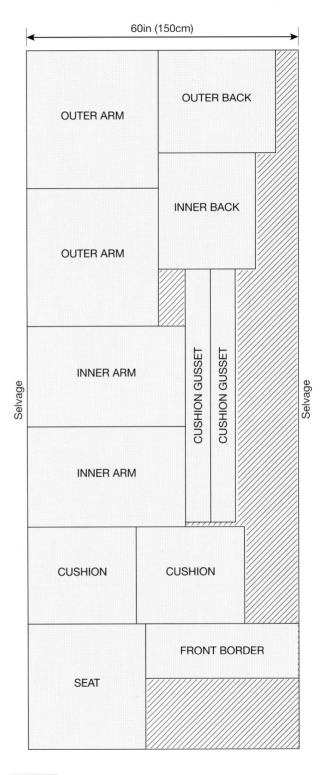

FIGURE 2 PLAN THE LAYOUT ON PAPER, BUT REMEMBER TO ALLOW FOR ANY PATTERN REPEAT, WHICH IS NOT SHOWN HERE.

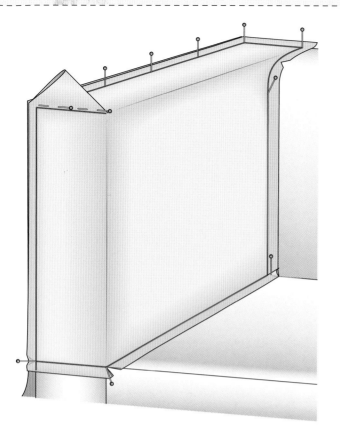

FIGURE 3 MARK THE SEAM LINES ON ALL THE PANELS IN THE SAME WAY AS FOR THE INNER ARM, SHOWN HERE.

5 Carefully remove the fabric panels from the chair.

CUTTING OUT

Smooth the fabric out on a flat surface, right side up. Lay out all the pattern pieces. Some can be placed side by side, but take care to position the pattern to best effect and match it where necessary (see p. 123). Cut out and label all the fabric panels. Transfer the seam lines to the fabric using chalk or fade-away pen.

SEWING SENSE

Check that the marker pen does fade or dissolve on a fabric scrap before marking the main fabric.

PINNING THE PANELS TOGETHER

Before doing any sewing, check the fit of the cover by pinning the panels together. Then you can adjust the fit as necessary.

EXPERT TIP

USE DARK-COLOURED GLASS-HEADED PINS ON PALE FABRIC AND PALE ONES ON DARK FABRICS SO THEY ARE EASIER TO SEE AND REMOVE LATER.

1 Pin the seat panel in position, right side down on the chair, keeping the grainline straight and the pattern level, especially along the front edge.

2 Pin the outer arm panel to the chair, again keeping it in line along the top edge.

3 Line up the inner arm panel and pin it around to the front outer edge, keeping the fabric straight, not at an angle. Clip into the seam allowance at the front corner so it folds around the corner smoothly.

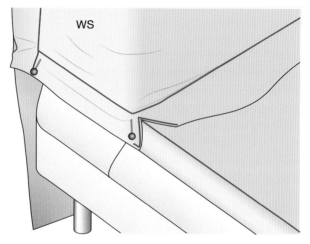

FIGURE 4 CLIP INTO THE INNER ARM PANEL RIGHT ON THE FRONT CORNER.

4 Smooth the inner arm panel over the top of the arm to meet the outer arm panel. Pin the panels together at the seam line along the top outer edge.

5 Smooth the inner arm panel towards the inner back of the chair, marking the seam line and clipping into the seam allowance at the top corners.

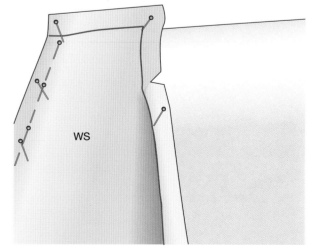

FIGURE 5 MARK THE SEAM LINE AND CLIP INTO THE CORNERS.

6 Pinch the excess fabric at the top of the front of the arm to form a triangle shape. Mark the seam line straight across the front edge of the arm and pin. Trim the excess fabric, remembering to leave a ¾in (2cm) seam allowance. Repeat from step 2 for the other arm panels.

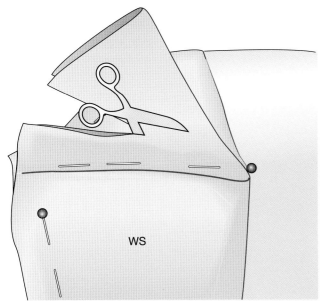

FIGURE 6 FIT THE INNER ARM ACROSS THE TOP FRONT EDGE AND TRIM THE EXCESS FABRIC.

7 Pin the top edge of the front border panel to the front edge of the seat and inner arm panels. Pin the outer arm panels to the inner arm and border panels down the front outer edge.

8 Position the inner back panel, making sure the grainline and pattern hang straight. Pin the bottom edge to the seat panel and the side edges to the inner arm panels.

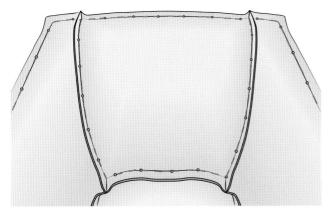

FIGURE 7 PIN THE INNER BACK PANEL IN PLACE.

9 Pin the outer back panel in place on the chair, making sure the grainline and pattern hangs straight. Then pin it to the top edge of the inner back and inner arm panels. Pin the side edges to the outer arm panels.

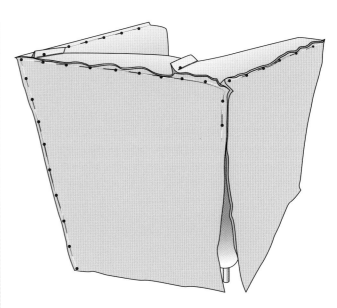

FIGURE 8 PIN THE OUTER BACK PANEL IN PLACE.

10 When all the panels are pinned together, check that the fabric lies smoothly, if necessary clipping into the seam allowances. Unpin any panels that need adjusting, smoothing out the fabric before re-pinning and, if necessary, marking a new seam line.

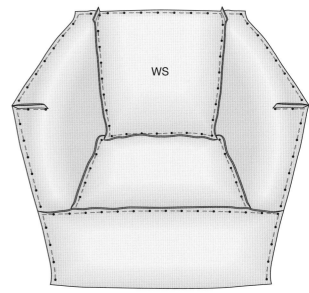

FIGURE 9 CHECK THAT THE COVER FITS PERFECTLY.

11 When you are satisfied with the fit, unpin an opening along one outer back side edge to within 3in (8cm) of the top back corner. Carefully remove the cover from the chair.

MAKING UP

1 If you wish, hand baste all the seams and remove the pins before sewing the seams. Otherwise machine them together, removing the pins as you sew. Use a regular straight stitch suitable for the fabric (2.5–3 length). It doesn't matter which seam you start with, but when you come to a three-seam junction, stop and decide which seam needs completing first to make the others flat. For example, sew the inner back to the seat and then to the inner arm, finally attaching the bottom of the inner arm to the seat. Remember to leave the opening on the outer back and side seam unstitched. Press.

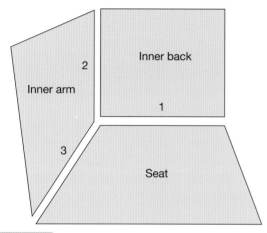

FIGURE 10 JOIN THE INNER BACK AND SEAT PANELS FIRST SO THE SEAM ALLOWANCES AROUND THE INNER ARM WILL LIE FLAT WHEN THEY ARE SEWN.

2 Neaten the raw edges on all the seams with an overlocker or by zigzag stitching (see p. 19). Press the seams.

3 Fit the cover over the chair, right sides out, lining up the seams along the edges of the chair. Pin the opening closed.

FINISHING THE BOTTOM EDGE

There are various options for finishing the bottom edge or panel of the chair cover. You can simply turn a straight hem or create a shaped hemline, like the scallops on the cover on p. 135, across the bottom edge of the existing panels. Alternatively, you can add a separate skirt panel, which can be trimmed, gathered or pleated as you please.

1 Fit the cover on the chair. Either mark a floor-length hemline or mark the seam line for a separate skirt all the way around. Remove the cover and lay it on a flat surface. Ensure the line is marked all the way around in one straight line.

2 If you want to hem the bottom edge, mark a further 4in (10cm) hem allowance below the hemline. If you are going to attach a separate skirt, add a ¾in (2cm) seam allowance instead.

HEMMING A STRAIGHT EDGE

1 Turn under 2in (5cm), and then 2in (5cm) again to create a double hem. Top stitch it in place from the right side, using either straight stitch and matching thread or using a decorative stitch and contrasting thread.

2 Press under the remaining seam allowances on the open back seam. Pin hook tape to the side edge and loop tape to the back edge. Machine stitch down both long edges of each piece of tape.

3 Close the tape and stitch across the top end through all the layers to prevent tearing when removing the cover. Press all the seams carefully.

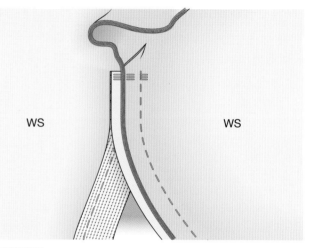

FIGURE 11 STITCH ACROSS THE TOP END OF THE TAPE THROUGH ALL THE LAYERS.

CALCULATING FABRIC REQUIREMENTS FOR A SEPARATE SKIRT

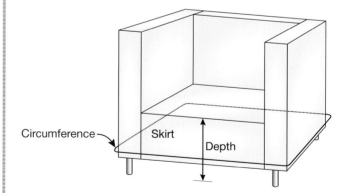

FIGURE 12 MEASURE THE HEIGHT AND LENGTH OF THE SKIRT.

1 Measure the height of the skirt from the front edge of the seat to the floor. Add 4¾in (12cm) for the hem and seam allowances. Then also add any pattern repeat necessary.

2 The length of the skirt will vary according to the treatment. Start by measuring all around the chair at seat level. Then add the following allowances for different treatments:

- for a straight trimmed or scalloped edge, add 4½in (12cm) for seam allowances
- for a gathered skirt, multiply the circumference by 2 for fullness and then add 4½in (12cm) for seam allowances
- for pleated corners, add 48in (120cm) for the pleats (12in (30cm in each) and then add 4½in (12cm) for seam allowances.

3 Work out how many widths of fabric you need by dividing the total length of the skirt by the width of the fabric. If the fabric has a pattern, the skirt length must be cut across the width of the fabric so that the pattern runs in the same direction as on the main chair cover. Multiply the height of the skirt, plus allowances, by the number of widths to give you the total length of fabric needed.

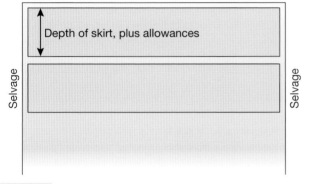

FIGURE 13 CUT THE PANELS TO MAKE UP THE LENGTH OF THE SKIRT ACROSS THE WIDTH OF THE FABRIC.

MAKING UP A SEPARATE SKIRT

1 Cut out the number of panels you need for the skirt. Join the panels along the short ends to get one long strip. Neaten the raw edges and press the seams.

2 Turn under ¾in (2cm) along the raw edges on each end. Tuck the raw edges to the inside, press and top stitch the hems in place.

FIGURE 14 HEM THE ENDS OF THE SKIRT PANEL.

3 Fold the skirt in half lengthways and mark the centre point. Repeat, to mark the quarter points. Each quarter mark will line up with a chair corner, with the opening on the back corner to match the opening in the chair cover.

4 Trim the skirt if you wish, lining up the trim parallel to the hem. Approximately 1½in (4cm) above the floor usually looks good. Stitch the trim in place along both long edges, turning under the ends and using matching thread.

5 Gather or pleat the skirt, as you wish. Gather each of the four quarters separately (see steps 3 and 4 on p. 69), pulling up the gathers until the skirt matches the bottom edge of the chair cover and the quarter marks line up with the corner seams on the chair cover. Alternatively, make one inverted pleat at each corner (see Making inverted pleats on p. 104), marking 3in (7.5cm) on each side of the quarter marks and then another 3in (7.5cm) further away. At the open back seam, make the pleat in two halves.

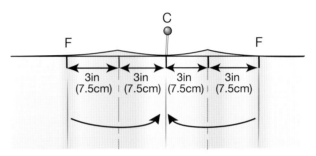

FIGURE 15 MAKE ONE INVERTED PLEAT AT EACH CORNER.

6 Attach the skirt to the bottom edges of the chair cover, matching the corners and taking a ¾in (2cm) seam allowance. Neaten the seam.

7 Turn under 2in (5cm), and then 2in (5cm) again to create a double hem. Top stitch it in place from the right side, using either straight stitch and matching thread or using a decorative stitch and contrasting thread.

FINISHING THE BACK OPENING

1 Press under the remaining seam allowances on the open back seam. Pin hook tape to the side edge and loop tape to the back edge, including the skirt. Machine stitch down both long edges of each piece of tape.

2 Press the tape together to close. Then at the top end, machine stitch across all layers to stop tearing (see Figure 11) and to strengthen the seam when fitting and removing the cover.

fabulous fitted CHAIR COVER

A FITTED COVER WILL FRESHEN UP YOUR ARMCHAIRS, OR SOFAS, AND GIVE THEM A STYLISH NEW LOOK. IN THIS PROJECT THE SCALLOPED EDGING ADDS A DESIGNER DETAIL.

FABRIC CALCULATION

The amount of main fabric you need will depend on the size of the chair, the width of the fabric and any pattern repeat. Therefore, before buying any fabric:

- take measurements of the chair (see p. 128), including the cushion, recording them carefully
- prepare the pattern pieces and, cutting the panels in calico, check the fit (see pp. 130–131)
- plan the cutting layout (see p. 129), taking the pattern repeat into account.

For the lining for the scalloped hem, you need a panel long enough to go all around the bottom edge of the chair (for more detail, see Finishing the scalloped edge, step 3 on p. 136), which can be pieced from shorter lengths.

YOU WILL NEED
✓ Calico for the pattern
✓ Furnishing fabric (as calculated above)
✓ Lining for the scalloped hem (as calculated above)
✓ 3–4 reels of matching general-purpose sewing thread
✓ Plate (to make scallop shapes)
✓ Hook and loop fastener as long as the height of the chair
✓ Pattern or parcel paper
✓ Buttonhole thread
✓ Basic sewing kit (see p. 8)

TECHNICAL KNOW-HOW
Taking measurements (see p. 128)
Preparing a pattern (see p. 129)
Cutting out (see p. 130)
Working with patterned fabric (see pp. 122–123)

CUTTING OUT

Cut out the main fabric only once you have drawn up a cutting layout (see p. 129) and checked that the pattern pieces fit the chair (see pp. 130–131).

1 Smooth the main fabric out on a flat surface, right side up. Lay out all the pattern pieces, excluding the cushion panels and gussets (see steps 1–4 on p. 137 for this stage). Some can be placed side by side, but take care to position the pattern to best effect and match it where necessary (see pp. 122–123).

EXPERT TIP

IF THERE IS A DOMINANT FEATURE IN THE PATTERN ON THE FABRIC, POSITION IT CENTRALLY ON THE MAIN PANELS OF THE CHAIR, FOR EXAMPLE THE INNER BACKS, AND/OR ALONG NOTICEABLE LINES SUCH AS THE HEMLINE.

2 Cut out and label all the main fabric panels. Transfer the seam lines to the fabric using chalk or fade-away pen.

3 Drape the panels over the chair to familiarize yourself with where they go.

PINNING THE PANELS TOGETHER

1 Before doing any sewing, check the fit of the cover by pinning the panels together, so you can adjust the fit as necessary. See Preparing a pattern on p. 129.

2 When you are satisfied with the fit, unpin an opening along one outer back side edge to within 3in (8cm) of the top back corner. Carefully remove the cover from the chair.

MAKING UP

1 Sew all the seams, following step 1 on p. 131. Remember to leave the opening on the outer back and side seam. Press.

2 Fit the cover over the chair, right sides out, lining up the seams along the edges of the chair. Pin the opening closed. Mark the hemline at floor level all around the chair. Remove the cover again.

EXPERT TIP

IF IT IS EASIER, MARK THE HEMLINE JUST AT THE FOUR CORNERS. THEN LAY THE COVER ON A FLAT SURFACE SO YOU CAN JOIN THE CORNER MARKS TO MAKE A CONTINUOUS STRAIGHT LINE.

3 Reinforce the corner seams by reverse stitching just above the hemline to prevent them ravelling.

4 Add a ¾in (2cm) seam allowance outside the hemline and trim the excess fabric.

FINISHING THE SCALLOPED EDGE

1 Measure the hemline across the front of the cover. Divide it equally to make a number of scallops. Working on the wrong side, draw around a suitably sized plate to mark the scallop shapes. Draw scallop shapes in the same way along the hemline on the other three sides, allowing for the seam allowances on the opening at the back.

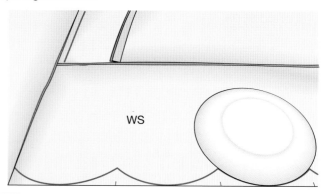

FIGURE 1 DRAW SCALLOP SHAPES AROUND THE BOTTOM EDGE OF THE FABRIC.

2 Mark a ¾in (2cm) seam allowance above the scallop line, following the curve. This is the sewing line. Cut the scallop shapes out along the lower line.

3 Cut a strip of lining long enough to go all around the bottom edge of the chair, adding ¾in (2cm) seam allowances at the opening edges. The depth of the strip should be twice the depth of the scallop to allow for the seam allowance and turnings. Piece the strip together as necessary and press.

4 Sew a narrow hem along the top edge of the lining and press. Pin and baste the lining to the chair cover, right sides together and matching the bottom raw edges. Then machine stitch along the marked scallop line.

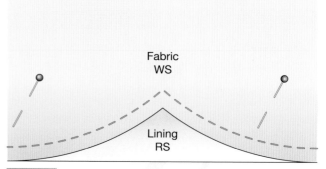

FIGURE 2 STITCH ALONG THE SCALLOPED HEMLINE.

5 Trim the seam allowance to ¼in (6mm), clipping into the corners of the scallops to help the fabric lay flat when turned through to the right side. Turn the scallops through and press. Top stitch the scallops ¼in (6mm) from the lower edge to hold them flat. Working on the wrong side, hand stitch the lining to the vertical seams so it will not fall down.

FINISHING THE BACK OPENING

1 Pin and stitch the hook and loop tape to both sides of the opening at the back of the cover.

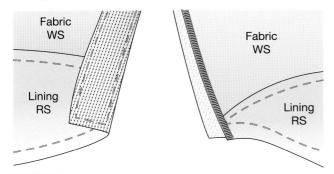

FIGURE 3 STITCH HOOK AND LOOP TAPE TO THE BACK OPENING.

2 Press the tape together to close. At the top end, machine stitch across all layers to stop them tearing and to strengthen the seam when fitting and removing the cover.

MAKING THE CUSHION COVER

1 Place the cushion on a sheet of paper and draw around the shape to make a pattern for the top and bottom panels.

2 Fold the cushion fabric wrong sides together and place it on a flat surface. Place the paper pattern on the fabric, centralizing any pattern. Mark around the pattern to give a seam line. Draw a ¾in (2cm) seam allowance all around, outside the seam line.

3 Cut out on the outer line to give a top and bottom panel. Remove the pattern and mark the missing seam lines. Mark the centre front on both panels.

4 Cut out the cushion gussets measured earlier. Join the pieces together at the short ends to make one continuous gusset. Mark the centre front of the gusset.

5 With right sides together, pin and then baste the gusset to the top panel, matching the centre marks and positioning the seams at one back and one front corner. Check that the cover still fits the cushion pad. Clip into the seam allowances at each corner to ease any puckering. Machine stitch the seam.

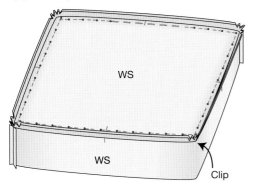

FIGURE 4 PIN AND BASTE THE GUSSET TO THE TOP PANEL.

6 Pin the bottom panel to the gusset in the same way, but leaving the back seam and 4in (10cm) of each side seam open. Machine stitch, trimming at the corners and clipping into the gusset so it will lay flat when turned through.

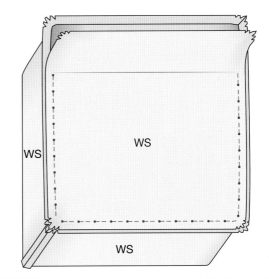

FIGURE 5 LEAVE AN OPENING AT THE BACK OF THE CUSHION COVER FOR INSERTING THE CUSHION PAD.

7 Press the cover and turn it through. Press the seam allowances on the open edges to the inside. Insert the cushion pad. Pin and then slip stitch (see p. 15) the opening closed. Place the covered cushion in the chair with the hand-sewn edge to the back.

> ### SEWING SENSE
> *Use a strong buttonhole thread to slip stitch the opening, but don't stitch too tightly so the stitches can be unpicked easily for laundering the cover.*

MORE DESIGN IDEAS
- Attach braid or fringing to the hemline instead of shaping it.
- Choose different coloured fabric for the outer and inner panels of the chair.
- Use plain fabric for the chair and a coordinating patterned fabric for the cushion, or vice versa.

GLOSSARY

APPLIQUÉ – additional fabric or motif attached to the surface of the base fabric, often stitched in place with machine satin stitch; see also Raw-edge appliqué, Reverse appliqué

BAGGING – a method of attaching a lining to the main fabric using the sewing machine to stitch them right sides together before turning through at the hem edge

BAR TACK – a number of stitches hand sewn on top of each other to form a definite stop

BASTING – temporary stitching to hold layers of fabric together

BATTING – also known as wadding; a soft spongy material made of polyester, cotton or silk and used to add bulk between layers of fabric

BIAS – the stretchiest part of the fabric, at a 45-degree angle from the selvage

BIAS BINDING – a folded fabric strip, cut on the bias of the fabric, that is wrapped around raw seam edges to encase them

BLIND HEMMING – a small stitch that is virtually invisible from the right side

BOX PLEATS – two symmetrical pleats folded away from each other to leave a flat panel in the centre

CASING – a channel through which elastic or a drawstring is fed to pull up the fabric

CLEAN FINISHING – a method of finishing the seam allowances on light- to medium-weight fabrics, by pressing under the raw edge and stitching it in place just through the seam allowance

CLIPPING – a method of reducing bulk around inner curved seams by snipping diagonally into the seam allowance close to the stitching

COUCHING – also known as gimping, this term describes yarns or cords stitched to the surface of the fabric

CROSSGRAIN – the grain running across the width of the fabric, at 90 degrees to the straight grain; formed by the woven weft fibres

DARNING FOOT – a sewing machine foot which does not rest on the fabric and is therefore useful for free-motion stitching

DOUBLE WELT SEAM – like a Welt seam, but with an additional row of stitching close to the seam line

EDGE STITCH – stitching that is visible on the right side of the fabric, sewn very close to an edge

EMBROIDERY HOOP – a two-part hoop that holds fabrics taut to prevent puckering when embroidering or free-motion stitching

FEED DOGS – jagged protrusions that come up through the throat plate on a sewing machine and move back and forwards to help feed the fabric through as it is stitched

FIBRE – the plant or synthetic substance from which a fabric is woven

FINISH – the surface treatment on a fabric, usually added after the fabric is woven

FLAT FELL SEAM – a neatened seam edge stitched wrong sides together with one seam allowance folded over the other to hide the raw edges

FREE-MOTION STITCHING – the term used when the feed dogs on a sewing machine are dropped and the operator controls the movement of the fabric under the presser foot, with the size and position of the stitches determined by the movement of the fabric

FRENCH CURVE – a tool that can be curved to fit a particular shape, for measuring and marking

FRENCH SEAM – a method of sewing a seam and encasing the raw edges of the seam allowance. The seam is sewn with the wrong sides together first, then refolded and sewn with the right sides together

FUSIBLE WEB – a light synthetic fabric with adhesive on one or both sides, useful for fixing hems or attaching appliqué shapes to the main fabric

GATHERING STITCH – long stitches sewn by hand or machine for the purpose of gathering the fullness of the fabric along the thread

GENERAL PURPOSE FOOT – also known as a straight stitch foot, a sewing machine foot suitable for all general purposes such as sewing seams

GIMPING – another term for couching

GRADING – a method of reducing bulk in a seam allowance by cutting each allowance to a different width

HAND OR HANDLE – used to describe how a fabric handles, drapes, folds and creases

HERRINGBONE STITCH – a useful stitch for sewing hems, which forms a criss-cross (or herringbone) shape on the wrong side of the fabric

HONG KONG SEAM – a seam where the allowances are wrapped with bias binding to conceal and protect the raw edges

HOOK AND LOOP TAPE – two complementary tapes that can be bought separately or together and used to fix two parts of a project together or fix a project to a solid surface; one tape has tiny hooks and may have adhesive on the back so it can be fixed to a solid surface; the other, which can be stitched to fabric, has tiny loops that fasten securely to the hooks on the other tape

INTERFACING – a layer of fabric or purpose-made fabric that adds strength and support to the main fabric

INTERLINING – a second layer of fabric that is attached to the main fabric to give it extra body and fullness

INVERTED PLEAT – two pleats folded in towards each other to meet in the centre

KNIFE-EDGE PLEAT – also known as a straight pleat; all the pleats face the same direction

LADDER STITCH – a method of stitching closed an opening left for turning a project through to the right side

LAPPED SEAM – a seam where the allowances are overlapped and stitched in place, which is useful for bulky fabrics that do not fray

LINING – usually lightweight, this is an additional fabric layer to add weight and richness to a project

LOCK STITCH/LOCKING IN – catching a tiny amount of one fabric to another using a single matching thread

MITRE – a neat finish to corners, achieved by stitching and cutting excess fabric on the diagonal from the corner

NOTCHING – a method of reducing bulk in seam allowances on outer curved seams; wedges are cut from the allowance so when turned through the seam allowance lays flat

OVERCASTING – a machine stitch for neatening raw edges

PATTERN – the design woven into or printed on the fabric

PATTERN PAPER – paper printed with a grid of lines or dots and crosses, for marking out patterns

PATTERN REPEAT – a pattern is repeated again and again down the length of the fabric; the repeat is measured from the top of the pattern to the top of the next identical pattern

PIN TUCK – a very narrow tuck of fabric that is stitched in place

PIPING – also known as welting, this separate raised edging defines the outline of a project; it can be a cord covered with contrast or matching fabric or a ready-made decorative cord with a flange

PLEAT – concertina folds in fabric to add decorative detail or control the fullness of fabric; see also Box pleat, Inverted pleat, Knife-edge pleat

PLEAT DEPTH – the total amount of fabric that makes up the pleat from the placement line to the fold line

PRESSER FOOT – general term for the different feet used on a sewing machine

PRICK STITCH – a tiny running stitch done by hand, which is barely visible on the right side of the fabric

RAW-EDGE APPLIQUÉ – additional fabric or motif, with the edges raw and unfinished, attached to the base fabric

REVERSE APPLIQUÉ – additional fabric or motif attached to the underside of the base fabric, which is then cut away to reveal the appliqué

ROTARY CUTTER – a cutter with a circular blade and handle that is excellent for cutting straight edges, and must be used with a self-healing cutting mat

RUFFLE – a separate length of fabric that is gathered and attached to the straight edge of another fabric section

SATIN STITCH – a very close machine zigzag stitch; the less the stitch width, the closer the stitches are together

SELF-COVERED BUTTONS – purpose-made metal or plastic buttons that are covered with fabric, to match or contrast with the main project

SELVAGE – the bound side edges of the fabric that run parallel to the straight grain

SERGER – a machine that sews seams, trims the seam allowance and overlocks the raw edges in one pass

SHEERS – transparent fabrics

SLIP STITCH – a small hand stitch used to hem lightweight fabrics by catching one or two fibres from the main fabric and then pulling the sewing thread through the hem allowance fold slightly to the left

STABILIZER – a layer of specialist fabric used to prevent the main fabric from puckering or distorting when stitched; various types are available, including tear-away, soluble and iron-on

STITCH-IN-THE-DITCH – a row of stitches worked within the seam of previous stitching on the right side of the fabric and used to hold facings, etc. in place

STRAIGHT GRAIN – also called the lengthwise grain, running down the length of the fabric; formed by the woven warp fibres

TAILOR TACK – a number of stitches hand sewn on top of each other and then cut between the layers of fabric to temporarily mark a particular position

TEXTURE – the tactile surface of the fabric

TOP STITCHING – stitching that is visible on the right side of the fabric

TUCK – similar to a pin tuck but slightly wider, these folds are stitched down the full length of the fabric; a number of tucks usually feature together

TWILL – a type of weave with a slightly raised pattern; the weft thread goes under two warp threads and then over two warp threads

VOILE – a lightweight, transparent fabric

WALKING FOOT – a sewing machine foot that helps to feed the top and bottom fabrics evenly, particularly useful for pattern matching and sewing thick fabrics

WARP – the vertical threads running down the length of the fabric, which were attached to the loom and lifted and lowered during weaving

WEFT – the horizontal threads woven across the width of the fabric, which were placed under or over the warp during weaving

WELT SEAM – suitable for heavyweight fabrics, the seam is stitched right sides together, one seam allowance is trimmed narrow, both are pressed to one side with the widest on top, then the seam is top-stitched through all the layers; see also Double welt seam

WELTING – another term for Piping

ZIGZAG STITCH – a machine stitch that swings from left to right

TEMPLATES

ALL TEMPLATES SHOWN AT 100%

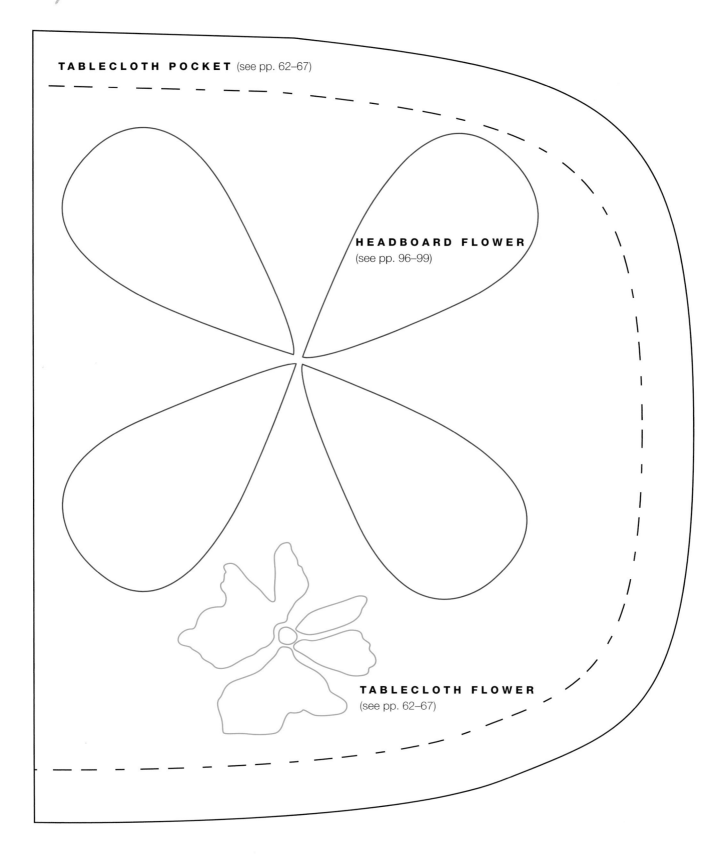

TABLECLOTH POCKET (see pp. 62–67)

HEADBOARD FLOWER
(see pp. 96–99)

TABLECLOTH FLOWER
(see pp. 62–67)

FABRIC SUPPLIERS AND CONTRIBUTORS

CHAPTER 1 – *Glitzy cushion cover by Wendy Gardiner*
Fabric: embroidered cream silk

CHAPTER 2 – *Kitsch kitchen chair cushion by Lorna Knight*
Fabric: Vanessa Arbuthnott, Raspberry spot and check (SC2)

CHAPTER 3 – *Designer director's chair by Wendy Gardiner*
Fabric: floral cotton canvas

CHAPTER 4 – *Delicious dining style table cloth by Lorna Knight*
Fabric: Abakhan Fabrics, Aqua linen and cotton blend (278965) and Vintage seersucker (280148)

CHAPTER 5 – *Seriously stylish seating by Pen Harrison*
Fabric: Abakhan Fabrics, cream celeste cotton

CHAPTER 6 – *Box clever bench seating by Pen Harrison*
Fabric: Vanessa Arbuthnott, Stripe and Dash (SD 16/14/6)

CHAPTER 7 – *Cone-shaped beanbag by Sue Locke*
Fabric: zebra stripe chenille

CHAPTER 8 – *Handsome headboard by Lorna Knight*
Fabric: cream sateen

CHAPTER 9 – *Beautiful tailored bedspread by Sue Locke*
Fabric: ribbon stripe polyester sateen

CHAPTER 10 – *Designer laundry basket liner by Sue Hazell*
Fabric: Vanessa Arbuthnott, Parterre in cranberry pink (PR12/11)

CHAPTER 11 – *Contemporary classic chair cover by Sue Hazell*
Fabric: green check cotton

CHAPTER 12 – *Fabulous fitted chair cover by Sue Hazell*
Fabric: Vanessa Arbuthnott, Feather and Egg in butter and sky blue (FE3/7)

ABOUT THE AUTHOR

Wendy Gardiner loves anything to do with sewing by machine. She has been editor and publisher of various sewing magazines for over 25 years and, for the last ten years, has been editor of *Sewing World*, Britain's leading sewing magazine. She has also written many books on sewing, written and presented six DVDs, including *Sew Easy, Dressmaking that's Fast and Fun* and *Sew Easy, Soft Furnishings*, and has recently uploaded several more sewing DVD clips on the Internet. She also co-manages isew.co.uk, a website packed with sewing advice, projects and techniques. Wendy is passionate about getting more people to sew and encouraging young people in this fun, affordable hobby.

INDEX

appliqué 46–51
   director's chair 52–57
   tablecloth 62–67

bags 91, 116–19
bar tacking 15, 87
basting 14–15, 18
batting 12, 82
beaded trims 30–34
beanbag 88–91
bedspread 106–9
bench seat 80–83
bias binding 19, 58, 59–61,
    67, 118
braid 30–33
buttons 22, 38, 39, 44, 45

casing 118–19
chair covers
   fitted 128–33, 134–37
   loose 124–27
   scalloped 135–37
   skirt panels 132–33
cleaning 26
cord
   in couching 9, 93
   piping 76–79, 100
   in ruffles 70
   in tucks 71
corners
   mitring 21–22, 31
   stitching 19, 22, 49
couching 93–94, 98–99
curves
   clipping 19, 59
   French curve 11
   stitching 47, 49, 58, 59
cushions
   chair covers 137
   glitzy 34–37
   kitchen chair 42–45
cutting
   fabric 11, 27, 123
   tools 10

director's chair 52–57

embellishments
   appliqué 46–51
   decorative stitching 92–95
embroidery hoop 94, 95
equipment 8–11

fabric
   bias 26, 40
   choice 24–27
   delicate 11, 15, 17, 19, 39
   grain 26, 40
   patterned 27, 120–23
   quantities 27, 122
   selvages 26
   stabilizer 12
   straightening 27
foam cube 72–75
free-motion stitching 94–95, 96
fringing 30, 32–33
fusible web 12, 47

gathering
   ruffles 69–70
   stitch 17, 18
grading seams 18

headboard 96–101, 142
hems
   blind 9, 15, 20
   curved 59
   double 20
   fusible web 12
   scalloped 135–37
   skirt panels 132–33
   top stitching 20
herringbone stitch 16
hook and loop tape 101, 132,
    133, 137, 139

interfacing 12, 46
interlining 12
ironing 12, 18, 19, 103

kitchen chair cushion 42–45

ladder stitch 16
laundry basket liner 116–19

lining 123
lock stitch 16

marking 11, 16
materials 11–12
measuring tools 11

napkins 62, 66–67
needles 9, 92
notching 19, 59

overcasting 19

pattern
   fabric choices 120–21
   matching 82, 123
   positioning 122, 136
   repeat 27, 122
pattern paper 12, 54, 129
pillowcase 110–11
pin tucks 71, 72
pinking shears 10, 12, 18
pins 11
piping 76–79, 80, 100
pleats
   box 104–5
   inverted 102, 104, 109
   knife-edged 102, 103
pockets 65–67, 102, 109–10, 142
point turner 12, 19, 22
pressing 12, 18, 19, 103
prick stitch 16–17

reverse appliqué 51
rouleau loops 41
ruffles 68–70, 74

satin stitch 47, 55
scissors 10
seam rippers 10
seams
   clipping 19, 26, 59
   curved 59
   finishing 18–19, 138
   French 112, 114, 116
   lapped 112, 115
   puckering 9

sewing 18
top stitching 112, 114
welt 112, 115
serger 12
sewing machine 8
   embroidery 92–95, 96
   feet 9, 21, 71, 87, 94, 99
   needles 9, 92
   stitching 17–23
   tension 9, 17, 95
skirt panels 132–33
slip stitch 15
stipple stitching 95, 98
stitching
   appliqué 47
   decorative 92–95
   in the ditch 20–21, 61
   hand 14–17
   machine stitching 17–23
straps 38, 40–41
stretch fabrics 19

tablecloth 62–67, 142
tacking 15
tailor tacking 15
tassels 30, 89
techniques 14–23
templates 142–43
threads 11, 92
ties 38, 40–41, 83, 127
top stitching 20, 34, 93,
    112–13
trims 22–23, 30, 31–34
tucks 68, 70–71, 74–75

wadding 12, 82
washing 26, 84

zigzag stitch 19, 47, 93, 95
zippers 9, 15, 83, 84–87, 88